Norwegian Mini Dictionary

ENGLISH-NORWEGIAN
NORWEGIAN-ENGLISH

FLUO
EDITIONS

FLUO
EDITIONS

Norwegian mini dictionary

© 2019-2020 by Fluo Editions

Main editor: J. N. Zaff
Assistant editor: Natalia Baena Cruces
Cover and typesetting: Fluo Editions

ISBN-13: 979-1-07-538771-5
ISBN-10: 1-07-538771-X

First edition: February 2020

Fluo Editions
Granada, Spain
efluo.net

Table of Contents

Abbreviations

n	noun
v	verb
adj	adjective
adv	adverb
art	article
pron	pronoun
conj	conjunction
interj	interjection
prep	preposition
part	particle
num	numeral
det	determiner
phr	phrase
inf	infinitive
sp	simple past
pp	past participle
m	masculine
f	feminine
n	neuter
pl	plural
abbr	abbreviation

English-Norwegian

abandon /əˈbæn.dn̩, əˈbæn.dən/ •
  n løssluppenhet,
  overgivenhet • *v* oppgi,
  skrinlegge; forlate; forvise;
  avskrive **~ment**; dereliksjon *m*
ability /əˈbɪl.ə.ti/ • *n* evne *m*
able /ˈeɪ.bl̩/ • *adj* i stand
abnormal /ˌæbˌnɔɹ.ml̩/ • *adj*
  abnorm, anormal, unormal
aboli|sh /əˈbɒlɪʃ, əbɑl.ɪʃ/ • *v*
  avskaffe, forkaste **~tion** • *n*
  abolisjon *m*
abortion /əˈbɔɹ.ʃn̩/ • *n* abort *m*
about /əˈbaʊt, əˈbʌʊt/ • *adv* rundt;
  nesten • *prep* rundt; om;
  omkring; angående; på veg til
above /əˈbʌv/ • *adv* ovenfor,
  over; høyere; over, ovenfor;
  utover
absolute /ˈæb.səˌluːt, ˈæb.səˌlut/ •
  adj absolutt • *n* absolutt *n*
absorb /əbˈzɔːb, æbˈsɔːb/ • *v* påta
  seg; absorbere; oppsluke;
  utholde
abstract /ˈæbˌstɹækt, ˌæbˈstɹækt/ •
  adj abstrakt; distrahert • *n*
  sammendrag *n*,
  oppsummering *m*, utdrag *n*,
  referat *n*, abstrakt *n*; ekstrakt;
  sammenfatning *m*;
  distraksjon *n*; abstraksjon *m*
~ce • *n* overflod
abuse /əˈbjuːs, əˈbjus/ • *n*
  misbruk *n*; utskjelling *m*;
  voldtekt *m* • *v* misbruke;
  mishandle; skjelle ut; voldta
academ|y /əˈkæd.ə.mi/ ; akademi
  n **~ic** • *adj* akademisk;
  akademiker *m*
accelerat|e /əkˈsɛl.əˌɹeɪt/ • *v*
  akselerere; påskynde; sette
  opp farten

A

accent /ˈæk.sənt, ˈæk.sɛnt/ ● n
aksent m, trykk n, betoning m;
uttale m, tonefall n; merke n ●
v aksentuere

accept /əkˈsɛpt/ ● v akseptere,
motta, ta imot; godta;
aksepetere **~able** ● adj
antakelig

access /ˈæksɛs, ˈækˌsɛs/ ; anfall n;
utbrudd n; besøksrett m;
aksess m; tilgang m ● v få
tilgang; aksessere

~al ● adj tilfeldig

~ly ● adv deretter

account /əˈkaʊnt/ ● n konto m;
redegjørelse m; forklaring m;
regning m

acid /ˈæs.ɪd/ ● adj sur; syre- **~ic** ●
adj syrlig

activ|e /ˈæk.tɪv/ ● adj aktiv

actual /ˈæk(t)ʃ(əw)əl, ˈak(t)ʃj(ʊ)əl/
● adj faktisk, reell, virkelig **~ly**
● adv for øyeblikket, reelt sett

ad ▷ ADVERTISEMENT

add /æd/ ● v legge til; addere

addiction /əˈdɪkʃən/ ● n
avhengighet

additi|on /əˈdɪʃən/ ● n tillegg n;
addisjon m, pluss n

address /əˈdɪɛs, ˈædɪɛs/ ● n
adresse

adequate /ˈæ.də.kwɪt, ˈæ.dəˌkweɪt/
● adj adekvat, tilstrekkelig

adjacent /əˈdʒeɪ.sənt/ ● adj
nabo-, ved siden av;
foregående, forutgående,
etterfølgende, følgende,
påfølgende, neste, motsatt

adjust /əˈdʒʌst/ ● v justere, stille;
korrigere

admiration /ˌæd.mə'eɪʃ.ən/ ● n
beundring

admi|t /ədˈmɪt/ ● v slippe inn

adult /ˈæd.ʌlt, əˈdʌlt/ ● n voksen
~ery ● n hor n

advance /ədˈvɑːns, ədˈvæns/ ;
forskudd

adventurous /ædˈvɛn.tʃɚ.ʌs/ ● adj
eventyrlysten

adverse /ˈæd.və(ɹ)s/ ● adj
ugunstig, uhensiktsmessig;
motstående

advertisement /ədˈvɜːtɪsmənt,
ˈædvɚˌtaɪzmənt/ ● n reklame
annonse

advice /ədˈvaɪs, ædˈvaɪs/ ● n råd n

advis|e /ədˈvaɪz/ ● v råde **~or** ● n
rådgiver m, veileder m

affect /əˈfɛkt/ ● n affekt m ● v
influere, gå utover; affektere

afford /əˈfoɹd, əˈfɔːd/ ● v tåle, ha
råd til; skaffe

Afghanistan ● n Afghanistan

afraid /əˈfɹeɪd/ ● adj redd,
engstelig

~n ● adj afrikansk

after /ˈæf.tə(ɹ), ˈæf.tɚ/ ● adv
senere, etterpå, etter ● prep
etter, bak; etter at **~noon** ● n
ettermiddag m **~wards** ● adv i
etterkant, derpå

against /əˈɡɛnst, əˈɡeɪnst/ ● prep
mot; imot

of ~ ● phr myndig

agenda /əˈdʒɛn.də/ ● n agenda m

agen|t /ˈeɪ.dʒənt/ ● n agent m;
spion m

~ve ● adj aggressiv

agil|e /ˈædʒ.aɪl/ ● adj behendig,
ledig, smidig, sprek **~ity** ● n
spenst m

ago /əˈɡoʊ, əˈɡəʊ/ • *adv* siden

agree /əˈɡriː, əˈɡriː/ • *v* være enig; jatte **~ment** • *n* avtale *m*, samtykke *n*; enighet *m*, overensstemmelse *m*; kongruens *m*

agreeable /əˈɡriːəbl/ • *adj* behagelig *n*

agricultur|e /ˈæɡrɪˌkʌltʃə, ˈæɡrɪˌkʌltʃər/ • *n* landbruk *n*, jordbruk *n*

aide ▷ ASSISTANT

AIDS • *n* (*abbr* Acquired ImmunoDeficiency Syndrome) AIDS

~line • *n* flyselskap *n*

albeit /ɔːlˈbiːɪt, ɔlˈbiːət/ • *conj* selv om, om enn

alert /əˈlɜːt, əˈlɜt/ • *adj* oppmerksom, våken • *n* alarm *m*; advarsel *m*, varsel *n* • *v* varsle

Algeria • *n* Algerie

alibi /ˈæl.əˌbaɪ/ • *n* alibi

alien /ˈeɪ.li.ən/ • *adj* utenomjordisk *m* **~ate** • *v* fremmedgjøre

alive /əˈlaɪv/ • *adj* i live, levende

all /ɔːl, ɔl/ • *det* alle; hele • *n* alt **~ right** • *adj* ålreit

~ly • *adv* angivelig, visstnok

alley /ˈæli/ • *n* allé *m*, strede *n*

allow /əˈlaʊ/ • *v* tillate

allure /əˈl(j)ʊər/ • *n* drag *n*

alone /əˈlɒn, əˈloʊn/ • *adv* alene; bare, kun

already /ɔːlˈrɛdi, ɔlˈrɛdi/ • *adv* allerede

~ive • *adj* alternativ • *n* alternativ *n*

always /ˈɔː(l)ˌweɪz, ˈɔlˌweɪz/ • *adv* alltid, bestandig; hele tiden, konstant

amazing /əˈmeɪzɪŋ/ • *adj* forbløffende

among /əˈmʌŋ/ • *prep* blant, mellom

Amsterdam • *n* Amsterdam

analys|is /əˈnæləsɪs/ • *n* analyse

anger /ˈæŋɡə(r), ˈæŋɡər/ • *n* sinne *n*

Angola • *n* Angola

angry /ˈæŋ.ɡri/ • *adj* sint

animal /ˈænɪməl/ • *adj* dyrisk • *n* dyr

anniversary /ˌænɪˈvɜːs(ə)ri, ˌænɪˈvɝs(ə)ri/ • *n* årsdag *m*, jubileum *n*; bryllupsdag *m*

announcement /əˈnaʊns.mɛnt/ • *n* bekjentgørelse

annoy|ed /əˈnɔɪd/ • *adj* irritert, forarget, forbannet, ergerlig **~ing** • *v* irriterende, plagsom, brysom, enerverende

another /əˈnʌ.ðə(r), əˈnʌ.ðər/ • *det* enda

answer /ˈɑːn.sə, ˈæn.sər/ • *n* svar *n*; løsning *m* • *v* svare, svar *f*; oppfylle, tilfredsstille

anxiety /æŋ(g)ˈzaɪ.ə.ti/ • *n* angst

any|one /ˈɛniˌwʌn/ • *pron* noen, enhver, hvem som helst **~way** • *adv* uansett

~ize • *v* beklage

apparently /əˈparəntli, əˈpærˌɛnt.li/ • *adv* tilsynelatende

appetite /ˈæp.əˌtaɪt/ • *n* matlyst *m*, appetitt *m*

apple /ˈæp.əl/ • *n* eple *n*; epletre *n*

applica|nt /'æp.lə.kɪnt/ • *n* søker
~tion • *n* program *n*,
applikasjon *m*; søknad
appl|y /ə'plaɪ/ ; søke
appreciate /ə'pɹiː.ʃi.eɪt/ ;
verdsette; forstå; stige i verdi
approach /ə'pɹoʊtʃ, ə'pɹoʊtʃ/ • *n*
tilstundelse, archaic);
innkjøring; tilnærmelsesmåte
m; innflyging
appropriate /ə'pɹoʊ.pɹiː.ɪt,
ə'pɹoʊ.pɹi.ɪt/ • *adj* egnet,
formålstjenlig, passende,
hensiktsmessig; velegnet • *v*
tilpasse; annektere
Arab • *adj* arabisk
arbitrary /'ɑː.bɪ.tɹə.ɹi,
'ɑɹ.bɪ.tɹɛ(ə).ɹi/ ; vilkårlig;
tilfeldig
~ure • *n* arkitektur *m*
area /'ɛəɹɪə, 'æɹ.i.ə/ ; område *n*
Argentina • *n* Argentina
arisen (*pp*) ▷ ARISE
arm /ɑːm, ɑɹm/ • *n* arm
arose (*sp*) ▷ ARISE
arrange /ə'ɹeɪndʒ/ • *v* ordne
arriv|e /ə'ɹaɪv/ • *v* ankomme
arrogan|t /'æɹəgənt/ • *adj*
arrogant
arrow /'æɹ.oʊ, 'æɹ.oʊ/ • *n* pil
art /ɑːt, ɑɹt/ ; kunst
article /'ɑːtɪkəl, 'ɑɹtɪkəl/ ; artikkel
m
articulation /ɑːˌtɪk.jə'leɪ.ʃən,
ɑɹˌtɪk.jə'leɪ.ʃən/ • *n* artikulasjon
m
artifact /'ɑːtɪfækt, 'ɑɹtɪfækt/ • *n*
kulturgjenstand
as /æz, əz/ • *adv* like • *conj* som;
når, da, idet; mens; siden

ascertain /ˌæsə'teɪn, ˌæsɚ'teɪn/ • *v*
fastslå
ash /'æʃ/ ; ask *m*
Asia • *n* Asia **~n** • *n* asiat
ask /'ɑːsk, 'ask/ ; be om
ass /æs/ • *n* esel *n*, asen *n*; idiot
m, tulling *m*, dumskalle *m*,
tosk *m*; ræv *f*, rumpe *m*
assault /ə'sɔːlt, ə'sʌlt/ • *n* voldta
assembly /ə'sɛmb.lɪ, ə'sɛmb.li/ • *n*
forsamling *m*
astronom|y /ə'stɹɑnəˌmi/ • *n*
astronomi *m*
asylum /ə'saɪləm/ • *n* asyl
ate (*sp*) ▷ EAT
athlet|e /'æθ.liːt, 'æθ.lit/ ; atlet *m*;
spreking *m*
atmosphere /'æt.məsˌfɪə(ɹ),
'ætməsˌfɪɹ/ ; stemning
atrocity • *n* grusomhet
attachment /ə'tætʃmənt/ ; utlegg
n, ta utlegg i
~er • *n* angriper *m*; spiss *m*
attain /ə'teɪn/ • *v* oppnå
attempt /ə'tɛmpt/ • *n* forsøk *n*;
angrep *n* • *v* forsøke, prøve
attracti|ve /ə'tɹæktɪv/ • *adj*
attraktiv, tiltrekkende;
tiltalende
attribute /'ætɹɪbjuːt, 'ætɹɪˌbjut/ • *n*
attributt *m*, egenskap *m*
audience /'ɔːdi.əns/ • *n* publikum
n; lesere
audit /ɔːdɪt/ • *n* revisjon *m*,
regnskapskontroll *m*,
bokettersyn *n*
aunt /ɑ(ː)nt, ænt/ • *n* tante *f*,
faster, moster
Australia • *n* Australia **~n** • *adj*
australsk

authorize /ˈɔːθəɹaɪz, ˈɑθəɹaɪz/ • *v*
bemyndige, gi fullmakt

automati|c /ˌɔːtəˈmætɪk, ˌɔtəˈmætɪk/ • *adj* automatisk

avoid /əˈvɔɪd/ • *v* unngå

awaked *(sp/pp)* ▷ AWAKE

awareness /əˈwɛɹnəs, əˈwɛənəs/ • *n* oppmerksomhet

awful /ˈɔːfʊl, ˈɔfəl/ • *adj* grusom, forferdelig

awkward /ˈɔːkwəd, ˈɔkwəd/ • *adj* klumsete, klønete; pinlig

awoke *(sp)* ▷ AWAKE

awoken *(pp)* ▷ AWAKE

B

back /bæk/ • *adv* tilbake • *n* bakside; bakende *m*; back *m*; rygg *m*, bak *n* **~bone**; ryggrad *f*

bad /bæd, bæːd/ • *adj* dårlig; gal; ubehagelig; ond; i stykker

bag /bæg, bæːg/ ; pose *m*; burugle; bagge

Bahamas • *n* Bahamas

Bahrain • *n* Bahrain

bakery /ˈbeɪ.kə.ɹi/ • *n* bakeri

balance /ˈbæləns/ • *n* balanse *m*; vekt *f* • *v* balansere

balloon /bəˈluːn/ • *n* ballong *m*; luftballong *m*, luftskip *n*

ballot /ˈbalət, ˈbælət/ • *n* stemmeseddel *m*; valgliste; opptelling *m*

ban /bæn/ • *n* utvisning *f*, forvisning *f* • *v* forby, utelukke

banana /bəˈnɑːnə, bəˈnænə/ • *n* banan *m*; bananplante *f*

band /bænd/ • *n* band *n*, bånd *n*; bind *n*; korps *n*; bande *m* • *v* binde; ringmerke

bang /bæŋ(g)/ ; pannelugg *m*, lugg *m*

Bangladesh • *n* Bangladesh

bank /bæŋk/ • *n* bank *m*; banke *m*

bankrupt /ˈbæŋ.kɹəpt, ˈbæŋk.ɹəpt/ • *v* konkurs, bankerott, insolvent

banner /ˈbænə, ˈbænə/ • *n* flagg *n*; banner *m*; fane *m*

bar /bɑː, bɑɹ/ • *n* bar *m*; skranke, bom; -bar *m*

Barbados • *n* Barbados

~ly • *adv* så vidt; nesten ikke

barn /bɑːn/ • *n* låve *m*

base /beɪs/ ; hovedkvarter *n*; frie

basket /ˈbɑːskɪt, ˈbæskɪt/ • *n* kurv *m*

bass /beɪs/ • *n* bass

bat /bæt/ ; balltre *n*

bath /bɑːθ, bɐːθ/ • *n* badekar *n*; bad *n*; bade **~room** • *n* bad *n*, baderom

bay /beɪ/ • *n* laurbær *m*; laurbærblad *n*; bukt *f*

bean /biːn/ • *n* bønne

bear /bɛə(ɹ), bɛəɹ/ • *v* (*sp* bore, *pp* borne) bære; føre; tåle, utstå

beat /biːt/ • *v* (*sp* beat, *pp* beaten) slå

beaten *(pp)* ▷ BEAT

~ify • *v* forskjønne

became *(sp)* ▷ BECOME

B

become /bɪˈkʌm, bɪˈkɒm/ ; kle
bed /bɛd, beːd/ • *n* seng *m*; bunn
   m; banke *m*; bed *n*
bee /bi, biː/ • *n* bie *f* ~**hive** • *n*
   bikube
been *(pp)* ▷ BE
beer /bɪə(ɹ), bɪə/ • *n* øl
beetle /ˈbiːtəl/ • *n* bille *m*
before /bɪˈfɔː, bəˈfɔɹ/ • *adv* før
began *(sp)* ▷ BEGIN
begin /bɪˈɡɪn/ • *v* (*sp* began, *pp*
   begun) begynne
begun *(pp)* ▷ BEGIN
behav|e /bɪˈheɪv/ • *v* oppføre
   ~**ior**; oppførsel
behaviour *(British)* ▷ BEHAVIOR
behind /bɪˈhaɪnd, biːˌhaɪnd/ • *n*
   bakpart *m*; bak *m*, rompe •
   prep bak; stå bak
Beijing • *n* Beijing, Peking,
   Pekin
being /ˈbiːɪŋ, ˈbiɪŋ/ • *n* vesen;
   tilværelse, det å være, bli til
Belarus • *n* Hviterussland,
   Kviterussland
belated • *adj* forsinket, på
   etterskudd
believe /bɪˈliːv/ • *v* tro
Belize • *n* Belize
bell /bɛl/ ; ringing *f*; innringing *f*;
   sjallstykke *n* • *v* henge en
   bjelle på
belligerent /bəˈlɪdʒ.(ə).ɹənt,
   bəˈlɪdʒ.ə.ɹənt/ • *adj* krigersk,
   stridslysten
belt /bɛlt/ • *n* belte *n*; region *m*
bench /bɛntʃ/ • *n* benk *m* • *v*
   benke
bend /bɛnd, bɪnd/ • *v* (*sp* bent, *pp*
   bent) bøye
beneath /bɪˈniːθ/ • *prep* under

Benin • *n* Benin
beseeched *(sp/pp)* ▷ BESEECH
beside /bɪˈsaɪd, bɪˈsaɪd/ ; på siden
besought *(sp/pp)* ▷ BESEECH
best /bɛst/ • *adj* best • *n* beste;
   best • *v* slå
bet /bɛt/ • *n* veddemål *n* • *v* (*sp*
   bet, *pp* bet) vedde; vedde på
betted *(sp/pp)* ▷ BET
better /ˈbɛtə, ˈbɛtəɹ/ • *adv* bedre •
   v forbedre • *(also)* ▷ GOOD
between /bɪˈtwiːn, bəˈtwin/ • *prep*
   mellom
beware /ˌbiˈwɛəɹ/ • *v* passe seg
Bhutan • *n* Bhutan
bias /ˈbaɪəs/ • *n* fordom,
   partiskhet
Bible /ˈbaɪbəl/ • *n* bibel *m*
bicycle /ˈbaɪsɪkl̩/ • *n* sykkel *m*
bidden *(pp)* ▷ BID
bike /baɪk/ • *n* sykkel *m*;
   motorsykkel *m*
bill /bɪl/ • *n* nebb; plakat
billion /ˈbɪljən/ • *n* milliard
bind /baɪnd/ • *v* (*sp* bound, *pp*
   bound) binde
bird /bɜːd, bɝd/ ; rype *f*
~**day**; fødselsdag *m*
biscuit /ˈbɪskɪt/ • *n* kjeks *m*,
   småkake *m*
bishop /ˈbɪʃəp/ ; løper *m*
bit /bɪt/ • *n* bitt *n*; bit *n* • *(also)* ▷
   BITE
bit|e /baɪt, baɪt/ • *n* biting *m*; bitt
   n; stikk *n*; tygge *m*, munnfull *m*
   • *v* (*sp* bit, *pp* bitten) bite på;
   bite
bitten *(pp)* ▷ BITE
bitter /ˈbɪtə, ˈbɪtəɹ/ • *adj* bitter
black /blæk/ • *adj* svart, sort;
   mørk • *n* svart, sort

blackmail • *n* utpressing *f*, utpresning *f*

blade /bleɪd/ ; blad *n*

blame /bleɪm/ • *v* skylde

blank /blæŋk/ • *adj* blank

blanket /ˈblæŋkɪt/ • *n* dyne *f*, teppe *n*

blast /blɑːst, blæst/ • *n* explosjon, sprenging

bled *(sp/pp)* ▷ BLEED

bleed /bliːd/ • *v* (*sp* bled, *pp* bled) blø

bless /blɛs/ • *v* (*sp* blessed, *pp* blessed) velsigne, signa, blessa

blessed *(sp/pp)* ▷ BLESS

blest *(sp/pp)* ▷ BLESS

blew *(sp)* ▷ BLOW

blind /blaɪnd/ • *v* blinde, blende

block /blɒk, blɑk/ • *n* kloss; blokk

blond /blɒnd, blɑnd/ • *adj* blond • *n* lys, blondine

blood /blʌd, blɔd/ • *n* blodsbånd *n*; blodprøve *m* ~**y** • *adj* jævla

blown *(pp)* ▷ BLOW

blue /bluː, blu/ • *adj* blå • *n* blåfarge **out of the** ~ • *phr* ut av det blå, som lyn fra klar himmel

blush /blʌʃ/ • *v* rødme

board /bɔːd, bɔːrd/ ; tavle, panel *n*; styre *n*; bord; vant *n* • *v* borde, entre, gå ombord; losjere

boast /bəʊst, boʊst/ • *n* skryt *n* • *v* skryte

boil /bɔɪl/ • *v* koke

bold /bəʊld, boʊld/ • *adj* modig

Bolivia • *n* Bolivia

bolt /bɒlt, boʊlt/ ; sluttstykke *n*

bomb /bɒm, bɑm/ • *n* bombe *f* • *v* bombe

bone /bəʊn/ • *v* pule, knulle

book /bʊk, buːk/ • *v* bestille, reservere; notere, nedskrive

boot /but, buːt/ • *n* støvel *m*

booth /buːð, buːθ/ • *n* bu

border /ˈbɔːdə, bɔːdə/ • *n* ytterkant *m*, kant *m*, rand *m*; bord *m*

bore *(sp)* ▷ BEAR

bored /bɔːd, bɔːrd/ • *adj* kjed

born /bɔːn, bɔːrn/ • *adj* født • *(also)* ▷ BEAR

borne *(pp)* ▷ BEAR

boss /bɒs, bɔs/ • *n* boss *m*

both /bəʊθ, boʊθ/ • *conj* både ... og ...

bother /ˈbʊðəɪ/ • *n* kluss, bry • *v* forstyrre, plage, irritere; gidde

Botswana • *n* Botswana

bottle /ˈbʊ.təl, ˈbɑ.təl/ • *n* flaske *f*

bottom /ˈbʊtəm, ˈbɑtəm/ • *n* passiv

bought *(sp/pp)* ▷ BUY

bowel /ˈbaʊ.əl/ • *n* tarm *m*; tykktarm *m*

bowl /bəʊl, boʊl/ • *n* skål *f*; skjeblad *n*

box /bɒks, bɑks/ • *n* kasse *m*, boks *m*, eske *f*, skrin *n*, øskje *f*, dåse *m*

boy /bɔɪ, bɔːə/ ; mann kar fyr; kamerat *m*, kompis

brain /bɹeɪn/ • *n* hjerne

brake /bɹeɪk/ • *n* brems *m*

branch /bɹɑːntʃ, bɹæntʃ/ • *n* gren *m*, grein *m*

brand /bɹand, bɹænd/ • *n* brennmerke *n*; varemerke *n* •

B

v brennemerke; innprente; stemple, stigmatisere

brave /bɪeɪv/ • *adj* modig

Brazil • *n* Brasil

bread /bɪed/ • *n* brød *n*

~ up • *v* slå opp

breast /bɪest/ ; bryst *n*; bringe

~feed • *v* amme

~e • *v* puste, ånde **out of ~** • *phr* andpusten

bred *(sp/pp)* ▷ BREED

bright /bɪaɪt/ • *adj* lys, livlig, lystig; glad

brilliant /bɪɪljənt/ • *adj* lysende, strålende; klar; enestående, genial; storslagen

~ sb/sth up • *v* oppdra

~cast • *n* kringkasting *f*, utsending *f*; program *n* • *v* kringkaste, sende ut

broadcast /bɪɔːdkɑːst, ˈbɪɔdkæst/ • *n* kringkasting *f*, utsending *f*; program *n* • *v* (*sp* broadcast, *pp* broadcast) kringkaste, sende ut

broadcasted *(sp/pp)* ▷ BROADCAST

broke /bɪəʊk, bɪəʊk/ • *adj* blakk • *(also)* ▷ BREAK

bronze /bɪɒnz, bɪɑnz/ • *adj* bronsefarget; bronse *m*, bronsefarge *m* • *v* bronse, bronsere

brother /ˈbɪʌðə(ɪ), ˈbɪʌðə/ • *n* bror *m* • *v* brors **~hood**; brorskap *n*

brought *(sp/pp)* ▷ BRING

brown /bɪaʊn/ • *n* brun

Brunei • *n* Brunei

BTW *(abbr)* ▷ BY THE WAY

bubble /ˈbʌb.əl/ • *n* bubla *f*

building /ˈbɪldɪŋ/ • *n* bygge, konstruere; bygning

built *(sp/pp)* ▷ BUILD

Bulgaria • *n* Bulgaria

bull /bʊl/ • *n* okse *m*

bullet /ˈbʊl.ɪt/ • *n* kule *f*

bunch /bʌntʃ/ • *n* bunke *m*; klase; gjeng *m*

burden /ˈbɜːdn, ˈbɝdn/ • *n* byrde *m*, belastning *m*; ansvar *n*

bureaucracy /bjʊəˈɪɒkɹəsi, bjʊˈɪɑːkɹəsi/ • *n* byråkrati *n*

burn /bɜːn, bɜːn/ ; brenning *m*; bekk, strøm • *v* (*sp* burnt, *pp* burnt) brenne; forbrenne; foræde

burned *(sp/pp)* ▷ BURN

burnt *(sp/pp)* ▷ BURN

Burundi • *n* Burundi

bus /bʌs/ • *n* buss *m* • *v* busse

bush /bʊʃ/ • *n* busk *m*

business /ˈbɪz.nɪs, ˈbɪz.nəs/ • *n* forretning *m*

busted *(sp/pp)* ▷ BUST

busy /ˈbɪzi/ • *adj* travel, opptatt • *v* sysselsette

but /bʌt, bʊt/ • *conj* men; enn; bortsett fra, unntatt, foruten

butt /bʌt/ ; bak *m*, rumpe *f*

button /ˈbʌtŋ/ ; trykknapp *m*, knapp *m* • *v* kneppe

buy /baɪ/ • *v* (*sp* bought, *pp* bought) kjøpe

by /baɪ/ • *prep* ved; innen; av; med; etter; for

bye /baɪ/ • *interj* adjø, farvel, ha det bra

C

cabbage /'kæbɪdʒ/ ● n hodekål, kål m

cabin /'kæbɪn/ ● n hytte f; kabin m

cage /keɪdʒ/ ● n bur n

cake /keɪk/ ; stykke m

calf /kɑːf, kæf/ ; legg m

call /kɔːl, kɔl/ ● v kalle

calm /kɑːm, kɑ(l)m/ ● v roe seg

calves (pl) ▷ CALF

Cambodia ● n Kambodsja

came (sp) ▷ COME

can /kæn, kən/ ; boks m, hermetikkboks m; do; rompe, bak m ● v (sp could, pp -) kunne

canary /kə'neəɹi/ ● n kanarifugl m; kanarigul

cancer /'kænsə, 'kæːnsə/ ● n cancer m

candid /'kæn.dɪd/ ● adj fordomsfri, upartisk; oppriktig

candidate /'kæn.dɪdət, 'kæn.dɪ.deɪt/ ● n kandidat

candle /'kændəl/ ● n lys

candy /'kændi/ ● n godteri

cannabis /'kænəbɪs/ ● n hamp

cap /kæp/ ● n skyggelue

capital /'kæp.ɪ.təl/ ● n kapital

car /kɑː, kɑɹ/ ; vogn m

carbohydrate /kɑːbəʊ'haɪdɹeɪt, kɑːɹboʊ'hɑɹdɹeɪt/ ● n kullhydrat n, kolhydrat n

carbon /'kɑɹbən/ ● n karbon n; blåpapir n; blåkopi m; kull n; kulldioksid m, kullsyre f

card /kɑːd, kɑɹd/ ● n kort n

care /kɛə, kɛ(ə)ɹ/ ; nennsomhet m

cargo ● n frakt

carriage /'kæɹɪdʒ/ ● n vogn m

carrot /'kæɹ.ət/ ● n gulrot

carv|e /kɑɹv, kɑːv/ ● v snitte

case /keɪs/ ● n kiste; hylster

cash /kæʃ/ ● n kontanter, penger

cast /kɑːst, kæst/ ● n gips m ● v (sp cast, pp cast) kaste

castle /'kɑːsəl, 'kæsəl/ ● n borg, slott

casual /'kæʒuəl, 'kaʒuəl/ ● adj tilfeldig

cat /kæt, kat/ ● v katte

catch /kætʃ/ ● v (sp caught, pp caught) fange

caterpillar /'kætəpɪlə(ɹ), 'kædəɹ.pɪləɹ/ ● n larve m

cattle /'kæt(ə)l/ ; bøling f, buskap m, fe n, krøtter, kveg n; stut m

caught (sp/pp) ▷ CATCH

cause /kɔːz, kɔz/ ● n årsak m, grunn m

ceiling /'siːlɪŋ/ ● n tak n

cemetery (British) ▷ GRAVEYARD

center /'sen.tə, 'sen.tə(ɹ)/ ● n sentrum n, midtpunkt n; midt

centre (British) ▷ CENTER

CEO ● n (abbr Chief Executive Officer) adm.dir

certain /'sɜːtn̩, 'sɨtn̩/ ● adj sikker, viss ● det viss f, visst n, visse, enkelte

Chad ● n Tsjad

chain /tʃeɪn/ ● n kjede n, kjetting m, lenke f; rekke f

~man ● n styreformann

challenge /'tʃæl.ɪndʒ/ ● n utfordring m

C

chamber /ˈtʃeɪmbə(ɹ)/ • n rom n, kammer n

chance /tʃæns, tʃɑːns/ • n sjanse m, mulighet m; tilfeldigheter; sannsynlighet m

channel /ˈtʃænəl/ • n kanal m

chao|s /ˈkeɪ.ɒs, ˈkeɪ.ɑs/ • n kaos

character /ˈkɛɹəktɚ, ˈkæɹəktə/ • n karakter

characteristic /ˌkʰæɹəktəˈɹɪstɪk/ • adj karakteristisk

charge /tʃɑːdʒ, tʃɑɹdʒ/ • n byrde m; pris m; ordre m; angrep n; beskyldning, søksmål n; ladning • v belaste, bebyrde; gi oppgave; saksøke

charming /ˈtʃɑː(ɹ).mɪŋ/ • adj sjarmerende

charter /ˈtʃɑːtə, ˈtʃɑɹtɚ/ • n pakt

chase /tʃeɪs/ • n jakt, forfølgelse • v løpe, forfølge; drive, punsle, siselere

chat /tʃæt/ • n prat m; chat m • v chatte

cheat /tʃiːt/ • n juksepave • v jukse, fuske; være utro, bedra; unngå, snyte, lure

check /tʃɛk/ • n sjakk m; kontroll m • v kontrollere, sjekke; krysse av, avkrysse; kryssjekke **~mate** • interj sjakkmatt

cheer /tʃɪə(ɹ), tʃɪɹ/ • n heiarop n • v heie **~ up** • interj opp med hodet • v muntre opp

chemi|stry /ˈkɛm.ɪ.stɹi/ • n kjemi m

chest /tʃɛst/ • n kiste f; kasse f; kommode m; brystkasse f, bryst

chew /tʃuː, tʃu/ • v tygge

chicken /ˈtʃɪkɪn/ ; kylling m; feiging m

child /tʃaɪld/ ; barn

children (pl) ▷ CHILD

Chile • n Chile

chill /tʃɪl/ • v avkjøle; kjølne; chille

chin /tʃɪn/ • n hake

Chin|a /tʃʌɪnə/ • n Kina **~ese** • n kinesisk m; kinamat kinesisk

chip /tʃɪp/ ; pommes frites m, pomfri m; potetgull n, chips m

chocolate /ˈtʃɒk(ə)lɪt, ˈtʃɔːk(ə)lət/ • adj sjokoladebrun • n sjokolade m; konfekt m; sjokoladebrun m

choice /tʃɔɪs/ • n valg

choir /kwaɪə(ɹ), kwaɪɚ/ • n kor n

chose (sp) ▷ CHOOSE

chosen (pp) ▷ CHOOSE

Christian • n Kristian **~ity** • n kristendom

Christmas • n jul f, jol f

churlish /ˈtʃɜːlɪʃ, ˈtʃɝːlɪʃ/ • adj bondsk; gretten

cigarette /ˈsɪ.ɡə.ɹɛt/ • n sigarett m, sigg

circle /ˈsɜːkəl/ • n sirkel; poser under øynene

circuit /ˈsɜː.kɪt, ˈsɝ.kət/ • n kretsløp n

circumspect /ˈsə.kəm.spɛkt, ˈsɚ.kəm.spɛkt/ • adj omstendelig

circumstantial /ˈsə:kəmˈstanʃəl/ • adj omstendelig

citizen /ˈsɪtɪzən/ • n borger

city /ˈsɪti, sɪti/ • n by m

civilization /ˌsɪv.ɪ.laɪˈzeɪ.ʃən, ˌsɪv.ə.ləˈzeɪ.ʃən/ • n sivilisasjon m

claim /kleɪm/ • *n* påstand *m*

class /klɑːs, klæs/ • *n* klasse *f*; kurs *n*; kull *n*; årskull *n* **~room** • *n* klasserom *n*

clean /kliːn, klɪn/ • *v* gjøre rent

clear /klɪə(ɪ), klɪɪ/ • *adj* fri; klar, ren; skyfri; gjennomsiktig

cleav|e /kliːv, klɪv/ • *v* (*sp* cleft, *pp* cleft) kløyve

cleaved *(sp/pp)* ▷ CLEAVE

cleft *(sp/pp)* ▷ CLEAVE

clerk /klɑːk, klɜːk/ • *n* kontorist, ekspeditør

clever /ˈklɛvər/ • *adj* klok, begavet, intelligent, skarpsindig, smart

cling /ˈklɪŋ/ • *v* klenge

clock /klɒk, klɑk/ • *v* ta tiden på

close /kləʊz, kloʊz/ • *v* stenge; lukke; avslutte **~d** • *adj* lukket

in the closet /ɪn ðə ˈklɒzɪt, ɪn ðə ˈklɒzɪt/ • *phr* i skapet

cloth /klɒθ, klɑθ/ • *n* stoff *n* **~es** • *n* bekledning *f*

cloud /klaʊd/ • *v* skye, overskye, formørke, fordunkle

clove *(sp)* ▷ CLEAVE

cloven *(pp)* ▷ CLEAVE

club /klʌb/ • *n* klubbe *f*; nattklubb *m*; kløver *m*; kølle *f*

cluster /ˈklʌstə, ˈklʌstər/ • *n* klase

coast /kəʊst, koʊst/ • *n* kyst, strand

coat /kəʊt, koʊt/ • *n* frakk *m*

cocaine /kəʊˈkeɪn/ • *n* kokain *m*

cod /kɒd, kɑd/ • *n* torsk *m*

coin /kɔɪn/ • *n* mynt *m*

cold /kəʊld, koʊld/ • *adj* kald; kaldt • *n* kulde *m*

collaborat|e /kəˈlæbəɹeɪt, kəˈlæbəɹeɪt/ • *v* samarbeide **~ion** • *n* samarbeid

Colombia • *n* Colombia

color /ˈkʌl.ɚ, ˈkʌl.ə(ɹ)/ • *n* farge *m*; fargetone *m*, kulør *m*; hudfarge *m*; koloritt *m*; fane *m* • *v* farge; fargelegge, male; rødme

colour *(British)* ▷ COLOR

combat /ˈkɒmˌbæt, ˈkɑmˌbæt/ • *n* slagsmål

come /kʌm/ • *v* (*sp* came, *pp* come) komme; ankomme

comic /ˈkɒmɪk, ˈkɑmɪk/ • *n* tegneserie *m*

commander /kəˈmændə, kəˈmɑːndə/ • *n* befalingsmand *m*

commence /kəˈmɛns/ • *v* begynne, påbegynne

comment /ˈkɒmɛnt, ˈkɑmɛnt/ • *v* kommentere **~ial** • *n* reklame *m*, annonse *m* **~ment**; engasjement *n*

common /ˈkɒmən, ˈkɑmən/ • *adj* vanlig

compar|e /kəmˈpɛə, kəmˈpɛə/ • *v* sammenligne **~able** • *adj* sammenlignbar, komparabel **~ative** • *adj* komparativ **~ison** • *n* sammenligning

compel /kəmˈpɛl/ • *v* tvinge

compensat|e /ˈkɒmpənseɪt/ • *v* kompensere

competition /ˌkɒmpəˈtɪʃən, ˌkɑːmpəˈtɪʃən/ ; konkurranse

compilation /kɒmpɪˈleɪʃən/ ; samling *m*

complaint /kəmˈpleɪnt/ • *n* klage *f*, innvending *f*

C

complexity /kəmˈplɛk.sɪ.ti/ ; floke *f*, forvikling *m*

complicated /ˈkɒmplɪkeɪtɪd/ • *adj* komplisert

~ition • *n* sammensetning

comprehen|d /ˌkɒmpɹɪˈhɛnd, ˌkæmpɹɪˈhɛnd/ • *v* dekke; fatte, forstå **~sive** • *adj* grundig, omfattende

comprise /kəmˈpɹaɪz/ • *v* bestå av, omfatte

conceal /kənˈsiːl/ • *v* gjemme, skjule, fortie, gøyme, dekke over

concept /ˈkɒn.sɛpt/ • *n* begrep, omgrep

concern /kənˈsɜːn, kənˈsɜːn/ • *n* bekymring; uro; konsern *n*, selskap *n* • *v* angå

concrete /ˈkɒnkɹiːt, ˌkɑnˈkɹiːt/ • *adj* konkret; betong-

condescending /ˌkɒn.dɪ.sɛnd.ɪŋ, ˌkɑndəˈsɛndɪŋ/ • *adj* nedlatende

condition /kənˈdɪʃən/ • *n* vilkår *n*; forutsetning *m*; tilstand *m* • *v* tilvenne; betinge **~al** • *n* kondisjonalis

condom /ˈkɒn.dɒm, ˈkɑn.dəm/ • *n* kondom *n*, gummi *n*

confess /kənˈfɛs/ • *v* tilstå; skrifte

configur|e /kənˈfɪɡ(j)ɚ, kənˈfɪɡ(j)ə/ • *v* konfigurere

confirm /kənˈfɜːm, kənˈfɜːm/ ; bekrefte

confus|e /kənˈfjuːz/ • *v* forvirre; forveksle; blande

conjunction /kənˈdʒʌŋkʃən/ ; konjunksjon *m*, bindeord *n*

connection /kəˈnɛkʃən/ • *n* forbindelse

~ousness • *n* bevissthet

consider /kənˈsɪdə, kənˈsɪdɚ/ • *v* vurdere; regne; betrakte

consistency /kənˈsɪst(ə)nsi, kənˈsɪstənsi/ • *n* konsistens

consolidate /kənˈsɒlɪdeɪt/ • *v* befeste

~cy • *n* konspirasjon

constitution /ˌkɒnstɪˈtjuːʃən, ˌkɑnstɪˈtuʃən/ • *n* grunnlov *m*, konstitusjon; helse *m*

consum|e /kənˈsjuːm, kənˈsuːm/ • *v* forbruke, bruke opp; fortære

contact /ˈkɒntækt, ˈkɑntækt/ • *v* kontakte

container /kənˈteɪnə, kənˈteɪnɚ/ • *n* beholder

contemplate /ˈkɑn.təm.ˌpleɪt/ • *v* vurdere

content /ˈkɒn.tɛnt, ˈkɑn.tɛnt/ • *adj* fornøyd, tilfreds **~ion** • *n* krangel *m*, strid *m*

contest /ˈkɒn.tɛst, ˈkɑn.tɛst/ • *n* debatt *m*, diskusjon *m*; konkurranse *m*

continent /ˈkɒntɪnənt, ˈkɑntɪnənt/ • *adj* kontinent • *n* kontinent *n*

contract /ˈkɒntɹækt, ˈkɑntɹækt/ • *n* kontrakt *m*, traktat, overenskomst • *v* sammentrekke, forminske **~ion** • *n* kontraksjon, forminskning; sammentrekning

~ory • *adj* motsigende

contribut|e /kənˈt(ʃ)ɹɪ.bjuːt, kənˈt(ʃ)ɹɪ.b(j)ət/ • *v* bidra

control /kənˈtɹəʊl, kənˈt(ʃ)ɹəʊl/ • v kontrollere, styre

convenient /kənˈviːnɪənt, kənˈvinjənt/ • adj praktisk

convey /kənˈveɪ/ • v formidle; overføre

cool /kuːl/ ; kald, rolig, behersket; reservert; cool, populær; stilig, kul; grei, ok • v hardne

cooperat|e /kəʊˈɒpəɹeɪt/ • v samarbeide

cop /kɒp, kɑp/ • n purk m

copy /ˈkɒpi, ˈkɑpi/ ; eksemplar • v kopiere; motta

cord /kɔɹd, kɔːd/ • n tau n

corn /kɔːn, kɔɹn/ • n korn n; liktorn

corpora (pl) ▷ CORPUS

corpus /ˈkɔːpəs, ˈkɔɹpəs/ • n (pl corpora) korpus m

correct /kəˈɹɛkt/ • adj riktig

corridor /ˈkɒɹɪˌdɔː(ɹ), ˈkɔɹəˌdɔɹ/ • n korridor m

Costa Rica • n Costa Rica

could (sp) ▷ CAN

country /ˈkʌntɹi, ˈkʊntɹi/ • adj landsens

course /kɔːs, kɔɹs/ ; rett m; rute f; bane m, kurs m; skift n

court /kɔːt, kɔɹt/ • n hoff n; domstol

cousin /ˈkʌz.n̩, ˈkʌz.ɪn/ • n fetter m, kusine f, søskenbarn n

cow /kaʊ/ ; ku f • v kue, underkue

crash /kɹæʃ/ • n krasje, sammenstøt

crawl /kɹɔːl, kɹɔl/ • v krype

crazy /ˈkɹeɪzi/ • adj galen, gal, gæren • n galning m, gærning m

cream /kɹiːm/ • adj fløte farget • n fløte; kremfarge; krem m

creat|e /kɹiːˈeɪt/ • v skape ~ion; skapning m

creative /kɹiˈeɪtɪv/ • adj skapende; oppfinnsom, kreativ

creature /ˈkɹiːtʃə, ˈkɹiːtʃəɹ/ • n skapning

credit /ˈkɹɛdɪt/ • n kreditt • v kreditere

• (also) ▷ CROW

crim|e /kɹaɪm/ • n kriminalitet m

criterion /kɹaɪˈtɪəɹi.ən/ • n kriterium m

critici|ze /ˈkɹɪtɪsaɪz/ ; kritisere

cross /kɹɒs, kɹɔs/ • n kryss n; kors n • v krysse

crow /kɹəʊ, kɹɔʊ/ • n kråke f • v (sp crowed, pp crew) gale

crowd /kɹaʊd/ • n flokk m, mengde m, folkehav n, folkemengde; haug m

crowed (sp/pp) ▷ CROW

crown /kɹaʊn/ • n krone; isse

cruel /kɹuːəl/ • adj grusom

cruise /kɹuːz/ • n cruise n

crush /kɹʌʃ/ • v sammenpresse; finknuse; sammentrykke; knuse ~ing • adj knusende

Cuba • n Cuba

cuckoo /ˈkʊkuː, ˈkuːkuː/ ; ko-ko n

cue /kjuː/ • n ku

cultur|e /ˈkʌltʃə, ˈkʌltʃəɹ/ • n kultur m

cup /kʌp/ • n kopp

curio|us /ˈkjʊəɹi.əs, ˈkjɜi.əs/ • adj nysgjerrig

current /ˈkʌrənt/ ; aktuell,
nåværende, gjeldende
cut /kʌt/ • *n* kutt *n* **~ sth out** • *v*
kutte ut **~ting** • *n* skjæring
cute /kjuːt/ • *adj* søt

D

dad /dæd/ • *n* pappa
dairy /ˈdɛəri/ • *adj* meieri-,
melke-; melkebutikk *m*;
meieriprodukter,
melkeprodukter
danger /ˈdeɪn.dʒə(ɹ), ˈdeɪndʒɹ̩/ • *n*
fare
dare /dɛə(ɹ), dɛɚ/ • *n* utfordring
• *v* våge; utfordre; risikere
~devil • *n* våghals *m*
dark /dɑːk, dɑːk/ ; mørk • *n*
mørke *n*
date /deɪt/ • *n* daddel *m*;
datering *m*; stevnemøte *n*,
date *m*; ledsager *m*,
noledsagerinne *f* • *v* datere;
sette dato; begynne med;
eldes **~d** • *adj* datert; foreldet,
utdatert; umoderne, utgått
daughter /ˈdɔːtə(ɹ), ˈdɔːtɚ/ • *n*
datter
dawn /doːn, dɔːn/ • *n* grålysning;
soloppgang
day /deɪ/ • *n* dag *m*, døgn *n*
deaf /dɛf, diːf/ • *adj* døv
deal /diːl/ • *v* (*sp* dealt, *pp* dealt)
dele ut
dealt (*sp/pp*) ▷ DEAL

dear /dɪɹ, dɪə/ • *adj* kjær; ærede;
kjære
death /dɛθ/ ; døden
debate /dɪˈbeɪt/ • *n* debatt
debt /dɛt/ • *n* gjeld *f*
decade /ˈdɛkeɪd/ • *n* tiår *n*, årti *n*,
dekade *m*, decennium *n*,
desennium *n*
decline /dɪˈklaɪn/ • *n* nedgang •
v avslå, avvise
decrease /dɪˈkɹiːs, ˈdiːkɹiːs/ • *n*
forringelse • *v* forminske,
forringe
dedicate /ˈdɛdɪkeɪt/ • *v* dedikere
deed /diːd/ • *n* dåd, gjerning
deep /diːp/ • *adj* dyp
deer /dɪə, dɪɹ/ • *n* hjort, rådyr
defeat /dɪˈfiːt/ • *n* nederlag *n* • *v*
overvinne, beseire
defence *(British)* ▷ DEFENSE
defend /dɪˈfɛnd, dɛˈfɛnd/ • *v*
forsvare, verne, beskytte **~se**
• *n* forsvar **~dant** • *n*
anklagede
defiance /dɪˈfaɪ(j)əns/ • *n*
motstand motvilje trass
deficit /ˈdɛfɪsɪt, ˈdɛfəsɪt/ • *n*
underskudd
definitely /ˈdɛf.ɪnt.li/ • *adv*
definitivt, utvilsomt *n*
degree /dɪˈɡɹiː/ • *n* grad *m*;
omfang *n*
delay /dɪˈleɪ/ • *n* forsinkelse
delegate /ˈdɛlɪɡət, ˈdɛlɪˌɡeɪt/ • *v*
delegere
deliberate /dɪˈlɪbəɹət, dəˈlɪbəɹət/
• *adj* med vilje; overveid;
veloverveid **~ion** • *n*
overveielse
deliver /dɪˈlɪvə(ɹ), dɪˈlɪvɚ/ • *v*
befri; levere

demand /dɪˈmɑːnd, dɪˈmænd/ • *n*
ettersørsel *m*; behov *n*; krav
n • *v* forlange, kreve

democra|cy /dɪˈmɒkɹəsi,
dɪˈmɑkɹəsi/ • *n* demokrati *n*,
folkestyre *n*

Denmark • *n* Danmark,
Kongeriket Danmark

~ial • *n* negasjon *m*; nekting;
benektelse *m*; fornektelse *m*

departure /dɪˈpɑːtjə(ɹ)/ ; avvik *n*;
bortgang *m*

deposit /dɪˈpɒzɪt, dɪˈpɑzɪt/ ;
depositum

depress|ed /dɪˈpɹɛst/ • *adj*
deprimert

desert /dɪˈzɜː(ɹ)t, dɪˈzəɹt/ • *n*
ørken

designation /ˌdɛzɪgˈneɪʃən/ • *n*
betegnelse *m*; benevning,
nemning

desir|e /dɪˈzaɪə, dɪˈzaɪɹ/ • *n* ønske

despair /dɪˈspɛə(ɹ), dɪˈspɛəɹ/ • *n*
frustrasjon *m* • *v* fortvile

dessert /dɪˈzɜːt, dɪˈzɜ̃t/ • *n*
dessert

deter /dɪˈtɜː(ɹ)/ • *v* forhindre;
avskrekke **~iorate** • *v*
ødelegge, skjemme, forverre;
nedbrytes, skjemmes,
forverres

devil /ˈdɛvəl, ˈdɛvɪl/ • *n* djevel *m*
~ish • *adj* djevelsk

dialogue /ˈdaɪəlɒg, ˈdaɪəlɔg/ ;
dialog *m*

diamond /ˈdaɪ(ə)mənd/ ; diamant

diary /ˈdaɪəɹi/ • *n* dagbok *m*

did *(sp)* ▷ DO

die /daɪ/ • *n* sokkel *m*; stempel *n*;
terning *m* • *v* dø, døy

differen|t /ˈdɪf.ɹənt/ • *adj*
forskjellig, ulik **~tiation** • *n*
differensiering

difficult /ˈdɪfɪkəlt/ • *adj* vanskelig

dig /dɪg/ • *v* (*sp* dug, *pp* dug)
grave; digge

digit /ˈdɪdʒɪt/ • *n* finger, tå

diligent /ˈdɪlɪdʒənt/ • *adj* flittig,
iherdig

dimension /daɪˈmɛnʃən,
daɪˈmɛnʃn̩/ • *n* dimensjon

direct /d(a)ɪˈɹɛkt/ • *adj* direkt • *v*
sette i scene **~ion** • *n* retning
f; ledelse *m*; produksjon *m*
~or • *n* direktør

dirt /dɜːt, dɜ̃t/ • *n* skitt *m*, jord;
smuss *n*, flekk *m*

disabled /dɪsˈeɪbəld/ • *adj*
bevegelseshemmet

disagree /dɪsəˈgɹiː/ • *v* uenig;
ikke stemme overens

disappear /dɪsəˈpɪə, dɪsəˈpɪɹ/ ;
fjerne **~ance** • *n* forsvinning *f*

disappoint|ed /ˌdɪsəˈpɔɪntɪd/ •
adj skuffet

disc *(British)* ▷ DISK

discharge /dɪsˈtʃɑːdʒ, ˈdɪstʃɑːdʒ/ •
n utvisning *m*; utskrivning *m*;
vannføring *m* • *v* utlade;
utskrive; losse

discipline /ˈdɪ.sə.plɪn/ • *v*
disiplinere

disclose /dɪsˈkləʊz/ • *v*
bekjentgjøre

discount /dɪsˈkaʊnt, ˈdɪskaʊnt/ •
n rabatt *m*

discretion /dɪsˈkɹɛʃən/ • *n*
diskresjon *m*

discuss /dɪsˈkʌs/ • *v* diskutere
~ion • *n* diskusjon, debatt *m*

dislike /dɪsˈlaɪk/ • *v* mislike

displacement /dɪsˈpleɪsmənt/ • *n*
deplasement *n*

dispute /dɪsˈpjuːt/ • *n* uenighet,
disputt *m* • *v* diskutere;
argumentere

disruptive /dɪsˈrʌptɪv/ • *adj*
splittende, nedbrytende

~ion • *n* distinksjon *m*; forskjell
m

distort /dɪsˈtɔrt, dɪsˈtɔːt/ • *v*
forvrenge, fordreie

distract /dɪsˈtrækt/ • *v* distrahere

distress /dɪˈstrɛs/ • *n* ubehag;
nødsituasjon

disturb /dɪsˈtɜːb/ • *v* forstyrre

divi|de /dɪˈvaɪd/ • *v* dele, delt på,
dividere

do /duː, du/ ; holde, holde for; gå
an; sitte inne, sone

dock /dɒk, dɑk/ • *v* kupere

documentary /ˌdɒk.jəˈmɛn.tri,
ˌdɑː.kjəˈmɛn.tɚ.i/ ; dokumentar
m

dog /dɒg, dɔg/ • *n* hund *m*, bikkje
f

dollar /ˈdɒlə, ˈdɑlɚ/ • *n* dollar *m*

dolphin /ˈdɒlfɪn, ˈdɑlfɪn/ ; dikkedal

domain /dəˈmeɪn, doʊˈmeɪn/ ;
definisjonsområde *n*

domestic /dəˈmɛstɪk/ • *adj*
huslig, hjemlig; husdyr *f* • *n*
tjenestejente *n*, pike *m*, tyende
f

done *(pp)* ▷ DO

door /dɔː, dɔɪ/ • *n* dør *m*

doubt /daʊt, dʌʊt/ • *n* tvil *m*

down /daʊn/ • *adv* ned; nede

~load • *n* nedlastning • *v*
laste ned, nedlaste

draft /drɑːft, dræft/ • *n* skisse,
utkast *n*, kladd *m*; dypgang;

trekk *m*; slurk *m*; verneplikt *m*,
tvungen militærtjeneste *m* • *v*
skissere, kladde; utskrive

drank *(sp)* ▷ DRINK

draw /drɔː, drɔ/ • *n* uavgjort;
loddtrekning *f*

drawn *(pp)* ▷ DRAW

dream /driːm, drim/ • *v* (*sp*
dreamt, *pp* dreamt) drømme

dreamed *(sp/pp)* ▷ DREAM

dreamt *(sp/pp)* ▷ DREAM

dress /drɛs/ • *n* kjole *m*; klær,
påkledning *m* • *v* kle; kle på
seg

drew *(sp)* ▷ DRAW

drift /drɪft/ • *v* daffe

drill /drɪl/ • *n* bor *n*; drill *m* • *v*
bore; drille; terpe; dypdykke

drink /drɪŋk/ • *v* (*sp* drank, *pp*
drunk) drikke **~ing** • *n*
drikking

drive /draɪv/ • *v* (*sp* drove, *pp*
driven) drive

driven *(pp)* ▷ DRIVE

drool /druːl/ • *v* sikle

drop /drɒp, drɑp/ • *v* slippe

drove *(sp)* ▷ DRIVE

drown /draʊn/ • *v* drukne

~mer • *n* batterist *m*,
trommeslager *m*, trommis *m*

drunk /drʌŋk/ • *adj* drita • *(also)*
▷ DRINK

dry /draɪ/ • *adj* tørr • *v* tørke

dug *(sp/pp)* ▷ DIG

dull /dʌl/ ; kjedelig; matt; dum •
v sløve

dust /dʌst/ • *n* støv *n*, dust *n*

dusty /ˈdʌsti/ • *adj* støvet

duty /ˈdjuːti, duːti/ • *n* plikt *m*;
avgift *m*

each /i:tʃ, itʃ/ • *det* alle, alt, enhver, hver enkelt

eager /'igə, 'i:gə/ • *adj* ivrig

eagle /'i:gəl/ • *n* ørn *f*

earth /ɜ:θ, ɜ̃θ/ • *n* jord *m* **on ~** • *phr* i all verden

easy /'i:zi, 'izi/ • *adj* lett, enkel; lett på tråden

eaten *(pp)* ▷ EAT

~ics • *n* økonomi

Ecuador • *n* Ecuador

edge /ɛdʒ/ • *n* kant *m*; sidekant *m*

edit /'ɛdɪt/ • *n* redigere **~or** • *n* redaktør *m*; editor *m*

eel /i:l/ • *n* ål *m*

eerie /'ɪi, 'ɪəi/ • *adj* skummel, nifs; engstelig

effect /ɪ'fɛkt, ə'fɛkt/ • *n* effekt *m* • *v* forårsake **~ive** • *adj* virkningsfull; effektiv; virksom **~ist** • *n* egoist

eight /eɪt/ • *num* åtte **~een** • *num* atten **~y** • *num* åtti

El Salvador • *n* El Salvador

elbow /'ɛl.bəʊ, 'ɛl.boʊ/ ; bend *n* • *v* albue seg

elect /ɪ'lɛkt/ • *adj* valgt **~ion** • *n* valg *n*

electronic /ˌɛl.ɛk'tɪɒn.ɪk, ɪˌlɛk'tɪɑn.ɪk/ • *adj* elektronisk **~ary** • *adj* enkelt

elephant /'ɛləfənt/ • *n* elefant *m*

elevator /'ɛləveɪtə, 'ɛl.ə.veɪ.tə/ • *n* heis

eleven /ɪ'lɛv.ən/ • *num* elleve

eligible /'ɛlɪdʒəb(ə)l/ • *adj* valgbar, egna

email /'i:meɪl/ • *n* e-post *m*, epost *m*; e-brev *n* **~ed** • *adj* flau

embassy /'ɛmbəsi/ • *n* ambassade *m*

emergence /ɪ'mɜ:dʒ(ə)ns/ • *n* emergens **~ze** • *v* understreke

empire /'ɛmpaɪə, 'ɛmˌpaɪ.ɪ/ ; imperium *n*

employ /ɪm'plɔɪ/ • *v* ansette

empower • *v* bemyndige

empt|y /'ɛmpti/ • *adj* tom • *v* tømme **~iness** • *n* tomhet

enclos|e /ən'kloʊz, ɪn'kləʊz/ • *v* vedlegge, tilføye

encourage /ɪn'kʌɪɪdʒ, ɪn'kɜ.ɪɪdʒ/ • *v* oppmuntre; anbefale

end /ɛnd/ • *n* ende *m*, slutt *m*; mål *n*, formål *n* • *v* slutte; avslutte, terminere **~ up** • *v* havne

enemy /'ɛnəmi/ • *adj* fiendtlig • *n* fiende *m*, uvenn *m*

energy /'ɛnədʒi, 'ɛnədʒi/ • *n* energi

English ; engelsk

enjoy /ɪn'dʒɔɪ, ɛn'dʒɔɪ/ • *v* nyte

enough /ɪ'nʌf/ • *det* nok, tilstrekkelig, fyllestgjørende • *interj* det holder! • *pron* nok

enter /'ɛntə(ɪ), 'ɛntə/ • *v* komme inn

enterprise /'ɛntəˌpɪaɪz/ • *n* foretagende

enthusias|m /ɪn'θju:zɪæz(ə)m, -θu:-/ • *n* begeistring

entirely /ɪn'taɪəli, ɪn'taɪɪli/ • *adv* fullstendig, totalt, komplett

entrance /ˈɛn.tɹəns/ • *n* entré, ankomst *m*; inngang *m* • *v* fortrylle, fascinere; sette i transe

entrepreneur /ˌɒn.tɹə.pɹəˈnɜː, ˌɒn.t(ʃ)ɹə.pɹəˈnəːr/ • *n* entreprenør *m*

~ious • *adj* misunnelig

equal /ˈiːkwəl/ • *adj* lik; er lik

equation /ɪˈkweɪʒən/ • *n* likning

equity /ˈɛk.wɪ.ti/ • *n* aksje *m*

erect /ɪˈɹɛkt/ • *v* reise; erigere **~ion** • *n* reisning *m* **~ile dysfunction** • *n* erektil dysfunksjon

escape /ɪˈskeɪp/ • *v* unnslippe, unnkomme; unngå

especially /ɪˈspɛʃ(ə)li, ɛkˈspɛʃ(ə)li/ ; spesielt

establish /ɪˈstæb.lɪʃ/ • *v* fastslå; etablere

Estonia • *n* Estland

etern|al /ɪˈtɜːnəl, ɪˈtɜːnəl/ • *adj* evig, endeløs, evinnelig

Ethiopia • *n* Etiopia

EU *(abbr)* ▷ EUROPEAN UNION

European Union • *n* Europeiske Union

evacuation • *n* evakuering *m*

evasive /ɪˈveɪsɪv/ • *adj* lukket, innesluttet; unnvikende

even /ˈiːvən, ˈiːvən/ • *adj* jevn **~ly**; likt

event /ɪˈvɛnt/ • *n* programpost *m* **~ually** • *adv* omsider

every /ˈɛv.(ə.)ɹi/ • *det* hver **~body** • *pron* alle **~thing** • *pron* alt, allting **~where** • *adv* overalt

~ce • *n* bevis *n*, evidens *n*; vitneutsagn *n*, vitneforklaring,

bevismateriale *n* • *v* vitne, bevise

evil /ˈiːvɪl, ˈiːvəl/ • *adj* ond, slem • *n* onde *n*, ondskap

evoke /ɪˈvəʊk, ɪˈvoʊk/ • *v* framkalle

exaggerate /ɛgˈzæ.dʒə.ɹeɪt/ • *v* overdrive

exam ▷ EXAMINATION

examin|e /ɪɡˈzæmɪn/ • *v* undersøke; eksaminere

example /ɪɡˈzɑːmpl, əɡˈzæːmpʊl/ • *n* eksempel, døme **for ~** • *phr* for eksempel

exceed /ɪkˈsiːd/ • *v* overskride; overgå, overstige

excellent /ˈɛksələnt/ • *adj* utmerket, storartet

except /ɪkˈsɛpt, ɛˈksɛpt/ • *conj* unntatt, bortsett fra, unnateke, unnateki • *v* unnta; unngå

excess /əkˈsɛs/ ; utskeielse

excit|ed /ɪkˈsaɪtɪd/ • *adj* spent **~ement** • *n* spenning *m*, opphisselse *m*

exclamation mark /ˌɛks.kləˈmeɪ.ʃən.mɑːk, ˌɛks.kləˈmeɪ.ʃən.mɑːɹk/ • *n* utropstegn *n*

exclude /ɪksˈkluːd/ • *v* utelukke, ekskludere

excuse /ɪkˈskjuːz, ɪksˈkjuːz/ • *n* unnskyldning *m* • *v* tilgi, unnskylde

exercise /ˈɛk.sə.saɪz, ˈɛk.sɚ.saɪz/ • *v* trene

exhaust /ɪɡˈzɔːst/ • *n* eksos *m*

exile /ˈɛɡ.zaɪl/ • *v* forvise

exist /ɪɡ'zɪst/ • *v* eksistere, bestå
~ence • *n* eksistens *m*,
tilværelse *m*

expan|d /ɛk'spænd/ • *v*
faktorisere; utvide,
ekspandere; utdype, greie ut;
vokse, bli større

expedient /ɪk'spi:di.ənt/ • *adj*
bekvemmelighet

expenditure • *n* forbruk *n*

expensive /ɪk'spɛnsɪv/ • *adj* dyr,
kostbar

experience /ɪk'spɪɹ.i.əns,
ɪk'spɪə.ɹɪəns/ • *n* erfaring *f* • *v*
erfare

explo|de /ɪk'spləʊd, ɪk'sploʊd/ • *v*
sprenge; eksplodere

exploit /'ɛksplɔɪt, ɪks'plɔɪt/ • *n*
bragd *m* • *v* utnytte

explor|e /ɪk'splɔ:, ɪk'splɔɹ/ • *v*
utforske

express /ɛk.'spɹɛs/ • *v* uttrykke
~ion; uttrykk *n*, mine *m*
~ve • *adj* omfattende /
omfangsrik

extract /'ɛkstɹækt, ɪks'tɹækt/ • *n*
ekstrakt *n* • *v* ekstrahere

exuberant /ɪɡ'zu:bəɹənt/ • *adj*
energisk

fabulous /'fæbjʊləs/ • *adj*
fabelaktig

face /feɪs/ • *n* ansikt *n*, fjes *n*;
mine *m*; anseelse *m*; flate *m*,
side *m*; kjeft *m* • *v* rett ut mot,
vende seg mot; konfrontere

fact /fækt/ • *n* faktum *n*

factor /'fæktə, 'fæktɚ/ • *n* faktor
m; årsak *m* • *v* faktorisere

factory /'fæktəɹi/ • *n* fabrikk *m*

fail /feɪl/ ; svikte; feile **~ure** • *n*
fiasko *m*, misære *m*

faint /feɪnt/ • *v* svime av

faith /feɪθ/ • *n* tro *m* **~ful**;
troende; tro

fall /fɔ:l, fɔl/ • *n* fall *n*; nedgang •
v (*sp* fell, *pp* fallen) falle; kaste
seg

fallen *(pp)* ▷ FALL

~ous • *adj* berømt

famil|y /'fæm(ɪ)li, 'fæm(ə)li/ • *adj*
skeiv • *n* familie *m*

fan /fæn/ • *n* vifte; fan *m* • *v* vifte

fantastic /fæn'tæstɪk/ • *adj*
fantastisk

far /fɑ:, fɑɹ/ • *adj* langt borte,
fjern • *adv* langt

fare /fɛə(ɹ), feɚ/ • *n* billettpris *m*

farm /fɑ:m, fɑɹm/ • *v* dyrke

fascination /fæsɪ'neɪʃən/ • *n*
fascinasjon, forheksing,
fortrylling; fascinert *f*,
forhekset, fortryllet

fashion /'fæʃən/ • *n* mote *m*

fast /fɑ:st, fæst/ • *adj* fast; dyp;
fargeekte; rask, kjapp; før, for
tidlig • *adv* fast; dypt; raskt,
kjapt, hurtig • *v* faste

fasten /'fɑ:sən, 'fæsən/ • *v*
spenne fast

fat /fæt/ • *adj* feit, korpulent
~al • *adj* skjebnebestemt;
skjebnesvanger, fatal

father /'fɑ:.ðə(ɹ), 'fɑ:.ðɚ/ • *n* far,
pappa, fader

fault /fɔːlt, fɔlt/ • *n* skyld *f*; forkastning *f*

favour *(British)* ▷ FAVOR

favourite /ˈfeɪv.ɪt/ • *adj* favoritt, yndlings

fed *(sp/pp)* ▷ FEED

feed /fiːd/ • *n* mating *m* • *v* *(sp* fed, *pp* fed) mate; leve av

feel /fiːl/ • *v* *(sp* felt, *pp* felt) føle, kjenne **~ing** • *adj* følsom

feet *(pl)* ▷ FOOT

fell *(sp)* ▷ FALL

felt *(sp/pp)* ▷ FEEL

female /ˈfiː.meɪl/ ; hunn- • *n* kvinne

feminine /ˈfemɪnɪn/ ; hunkjønn

fetch /fetʃ/ • *v* hente

fever /ˈfiːvə, ˈfivɚ/ • *n* feber *m*

few /fjuː, fju/ • *det* få, noen **~er** • *det* færre

field /fiːld, fild/ ; åker *m*; felt *n*; fagfelt *n*; kropp *m*; bane *m*

fierce /fɪəs, fɪɹs/ • *adj* voldsom

fift|een /fɪfˈtiːn, fɪfˈtiːn/ • *num* femten **~h** • *adj* femte **~y** • *num* femti

fight /faɪt/ • *n* stridslyst; slåsskamp; slag; kamp • *v* *(sp* fought, *pp* fought) kjempe for, slåss; bekjempe; kjempe

file /faɪl/ • *n* arkiv *n* • *v* arkivere; lagre; inngi

filter /ˈfɪltə, ˈfɪltɚ/ • *n* filter *n*

filth /fɪlθ/ • *n* skitt *m* **~y** • *adj* møkkete; slibrig

financ|e /ˈf(a)ɪˌnæns/ • *n* finanser

find /faɪnd/ • *n* funn *m* • *v* *(sp* found, *pp* found) finne **~ out** • *v* finne ut

fine /faɪn, fæːn/ • *adj* flott; fint; fin, bra; pen • *adv* fint, bra • *n* bot *m* • *v* bøtelegge, ilegge bot

finger /ˈfɪŋgə, ˈfɪŋgɚ/ • *n* finger *m*

finish /ˈfɪnɪʃ/ • *n* avslutning *f*, slutt *m*; toppstrøk *n*, finish *m* • *v* fullføre, avslutte

Fin|land • *n* Finland

fire /ˈfaɪ.ə(ɹ), ˈfɑɪ.ə(ɹ)/ ; bål *n*; brann *m*; fyr *m* • *v* brenne; gi sparken, sparke, avskjedige; avfyre; fyre **~work** • *n* fyrverkeri

fish /fɪʃ, fəʃ/ • *n* *(pl* fish) fisk *m* • *v* fiske **~ing** • *n* fisking *f*

fist /fɪst/ • *n* neve *m*, knyttneve *m*

fit /fɪt/ • *adj* deilig

five /faɪv, fäːv/ • *num* fem

fix /ˈfɪks/ • *n* skudd *n*, fix *m*; dilemma *n*, knipe; reparasjon *m* • *v* ordne; fikse; gjelde; fiksere; feste

flag /flæg, fleɪg/ • *n* flagg *n*

flamingo /fləˈmɪŋgoʊ/ • *n* flamingo *m*

flat /flæt/ • *adj* flat; monoton; -es; doven; dødt *n*

flavor /ˈfleɪvə, ˈfleɪvɚ/ • *n* smak

flavour *(British)* ▷ FLAVOR

fled *(sp/pp)* ▷ FLEE

flew *(sp)* ▷ FLY

flexib|le /ˈflek.sɪ.bəl/ • *adj* fleksibel

flood /flʌd/ • *v* oversvømme

floor /flɔː, flɔɹ/ • *n* gulv *n*

flour /ˈflaʊə, ˈflaʊɚ/ • *n* mjøl *n*

flow /flaʊ, floʊ/ • *n* flom *m*, strøm *m*; flo *m* • *v* flomme, strømme, fløda, fløyma

flown *(pp)* ▷ FLY

flung *(sp/pp)* ▷ FLING

fly /flaɪ/ ; gylf *m*; glidelås *m*; fly

fog /fɒg, fag/ • *n* tåke *f*; skodde *f*; dugg *m*; uklarhet *m*; uskarphet *m* • *v* dugge; tåkelegge

folder /fooldər, ˈfəʊldə/ • *n* mappe *m*

folk /fəʊk, foʊk/ • *n* folk *n*, befolkning *f*

follow /ˈfɒləʊ, ˈfɑloʊ/ • *v* følge

fond /fɒnd, fand/ • *v* være glad i

food /fuːd, fud/ • *n* mat *m*, føde *f*, næring *f*

fool /fuːl/ • *n* tosk *m*, dust *m*, tulling *m*; narr *m* • *v* narre, lure

foot /fʊt/ • *n* (*pl* feet) pote labb • *v* sparke; betale **~age** • *n* filmmateriale *n* **~ball** • *n* fotball *m*

for /fɔː(ɹ), fɔɹ/ • *conj* for, fordi • *prep* mot; til

forbad *(sp)* ▷ FORBID

forbade *(sp)* ▷ FORBID

forbid /fəˈbɪd/ • *v* (*sp* forbad, *pp* forbid) forby

forbidden *(pp)* ▷ FORBID

force /fɔɹs, fɔːs/ • *n* kraft *f*; styrke *m*; tvang *m* • *v* tvinge; påtvinge

forecast /ˈfɔɹkæst, ˈfɔːkɑːst/ • *v* (*sp* forecast, *pp* forecast) forutsi, predikere

forecasted *(sp/pp)* ▷ FORECAST

forest /ˈfɒɹɪst, ˈfɔɹɪst/ • *n* skog *m*

forgive /fəˈɡɪv, fəˈɡɪv/ • *v* tilgi, forlate

forgot *(sp)* ▷ FORGET

forgotten *(pp)* ▷ FORGET

formal /ˈfɔɹməl, ˈfɔːməl/ • *adj* formell

formation /fɔɹˈmeɪʃən, fə(ɹ)ˈmeɪʃən/ • *n* formasjon *m*

forsake /fɔɹˈseɪk/ • *v* (*sp* forsook, *pp* forsaken) forlate

forsaken *(pp)* ▷ FORSAKE

forsook *(sp)* ▷ FORSAKE

forthcoming ; imøtekommende

fortune /ˈfɔːtʃuːn, ˈfɔɹtʃən/ • *n* flaks

forty /ˈfɔɹti/ • *num* førti

forum /ˈfɔːɹəm/ • *n* forum *n*, fora

forward /ˈfɔːwəd, ˈfɔɹwəd/ • *adj* direkte; framtidig; fremre • *adv* framover, heretter; forward *m*; baug *m*

fought *(sp/pp)* ▷ FIGHT

found /faʊnd/ • *v* grunnlegge • *(also)* ▷ FIND **~ation** • *n* fundament; grunnmur

four /fɔː, fo(ː)ɹ/ • *num* fire **~teen** • *num* fjorten **~th** • *adj* fjerde

fox /fɒks, fɑks/ • *n* rev *m*

fraction /ˈfɹækʃən/ • *n* andel *m*, brøkdel *m*; brøk *m*

frame /fɹeɪm/ • *n* bjelkelag *n*, rammeverk *n*, armatur *m*; beingrind *f*; ramme *f*; frame *m* • *v* innramme

France • *n* Frankrike

frank /fɹæŋk/ • *adj* frank

fraud /fɹɔːd, fɹɔd/ • *n* bedrageri *n*, svindel *m*

free /fɹiː/ • *adj* fri; løs; åpen; ledig; uten • *adv* gratis • *v* frigjøre, frigi, befri, løslate **~dom** • *n* fridom *m*

freeze /fɹiːz/ • *v* (*sp* froze, *pp* frozen) fryse

French /fɹɛntʃ/ ; franskmenn

frequen|t /ˈfɹiːkwənt/ • *adj* hyppig **~cy**; frekvens *m*

fresh /fɹɛʃ/ • *adj* fersk **~man** • *n* første klasse, førstis

Friday ● *n* fredag

fridge ▷ REFRIGERATOR

friend /fɹɛnd, frɪnd/ ● *n* venn *m*, venninne *f*

frog /frɒɡ, fɹɑɡ/ ● *n* frosk *m*

from /frɒm, fɹʌm/ ● *prep* fra; fra; mot

front /fɹʌnt/ ; front *m*, fasade *m*

froze *(sp)* ▷ FREEZE

● *(also)* ▷ FREEZE

fuck /fʌk, fʊk/ ● *interj* faen!, helvete! ● *n* knull *n*, ligg *n*, nummer *n* ● *v* pule, knulle, jokke **~ing** ● *adj* jævla; forpult ● *n* knull *n*

full /fʊl/ ● *adj* full; fullstendig, komplett; hel; mett; vid **~-time** ● *adj* heltids

fun /fʌn, fən/ ● *n* moro **~ny** ● *adj* artig; rar, merkelig

function /ˈfʌŋ(k)ʃən, ˈfʌŋkʃən/ ● *n* funksjon *m*; post *m*, stilling *f*

fundamental ● *n* fundamental

funeral /ˈfjuːnəɹəl, ˈfjunəɹəl/ ● *n* begravelse *m*, jordfestelse *m*

furious /ˈfjʊə.ɹɪəs, ˈfjʊɹ.i.əs/ ● *adj* olm; med voldsom kraft

fusion /ˈfjuː.ʒən/ ; sammensmelting

future /ˈfjuːtʃə, ˈfjuːtʃɚ/ ● *n* framtid *f*

G

Gabon ● *n* Gabon

gain /ɡeɪn/ ; forsterkning *f*

galaxy /ˈɡaləksi, ˈɡæləksi/ ● *n* galakse *m*

Gambia ● *n* Gambia

game /ɡeɪm/ ● *adj* med ● *n* spill, lek

garbage /ˈɡɑɹbɪdʒ, ˈɡɑːbɪdʒ/ ● *n* avfall *n*, søppel *m*, boss *n*

garden /ˈɡɑɹdn̩, ˈɡɑːdn̩/ ● *n* hage *m*, have *m*; park *m*; tomt *m*

gasoline /ˈɡæs.ə.lin/ ● *n* bensin *m*

gasp /ɡɑːsp, ɡæsp/ ● *n* gisp *n*; drag *n* ● *v* gispe; pese

gate /ɡeɪt/ ● *n* port *m*

gave *(sp)* ▷ GIVE

gay /ɡeɪ/ ● *adj* festlig, glad, livlig; morsom, fargerik; homoseksuell, homo, homse, soper, bøg *m*; homsete; femi ● *n* homse

geese *(pl)* ▷ GOOSE

gender /ˈdʒɛndə, ˈdʒɛndɚ/ ● *n* kjønn *n*

general /ˈdʒɛnɹəl, ˈdʒɛnəɹəl/ ● *adj* allmenn, generell; alminnelig, vanlig

generic /dʒɪˈnɛɹɪk/ ● *adj* generisk; merkelø/s; kjo/nnsno/ytral

genocide /ˈdʒɛnəsaɪd/ ● *n* folkemord

gentleman /ˈdʒɛn.təl.mən, ˈdʒɛ̃.əl.mən/ ● *n* herrer, herretoalett *n*

Georgia ● *n* Georgia

get /ɡɛt/ ● *v* *(sp* got, *pp* got) få tak i, oppnå; få, motta; bli; forstå, fatte **~ over sth** ● *v* komme over **~ up** ● *v* stå opp

Ghana ● *n* Ghana

give /gɪv/ • *v* (*sp* gave, *pp* given) gi, overrekke, overlate, skjenke; gi etter

given (*pp*) ▷ GIVE

glasses ▷ SPECTACLES

glory /ˈglɔːɹi, ˈgloʊ(ː)ɹi/ • *n* prakt; glorie *m*, ære; pris *m*

glove /glʌv/ • *n* vante *m*, hanske *m*

glue /gluː/ • *n* lim *n*

gnawed (*sp/pp*) ▷ GNAW

gnawn (*pp*) ▷ GNAW

go /gəʊ, goʊ/ • *v* (*sp* went, *pp* gone) gå, virke, være i gang; forsvinne, gå over; ødelegges; reise, fare, dra; passe; ligge, høre til; gå ut med, date, være sammen med; si

goal /gəʊl, goʊl/ • *n* mål, målsetting, formål *n*, siktemål *n*

God /gɒd, gɑd/ • *n* Gud *m*, Herre

god /gɒd, gɑd/ • *n* gud *m* • *v* forgude, idolisere

golden /ˈgəʊl.dən, ˈgoʊl.dən/ • *adj* gyllen

gone (*pp*) ▷ GO

good /gʊd, gʊ(d)/ • *adj* god, godt; sunn; flink **~bye** • *interj* adjø, farvel, avskjed, hadet bra, hadet, ses, snakkes, hei

gorgeous /ˈgɔːdʒəs, ˈgɔɹdʒəs/ • *adj* smellvakker

gossip /ˈgɒs.ɪp, ˈgɑs.ɪp/ • *n* sladder *n* • *v* sladre, slarve

got (*sp*) ▷ GET

gotten (*pp*) ▷ GET

grace /gɹeɪs/ ; betalingsutsettelse *m*

grade /gɹeɪd/ ; trinn

grain /gɹeɪn/ • *n* korn *n*

grand /gɹænd/ • *adj* beste- **~daughter** • *n* sønnedatter, datterdatter **~father** • *n* morfar, farfar **~mother** • *n* bestemor, mormor *f*, farmor *f*

grant /gɹɑːnt, gɹænt/ • *n* tildeling *f*; innrømmelse *m*; donasjon *m*; overføring *f* • *v* tildele, overgi; innvilge; innrømme

grape /gɹeɪp/ ; vindrue *f*

graphic /ˈgɹæfɪk/ • *adj* grafisk

grasp /gɹɑːsp, gɹæsp/ • *v* begripe **~hopper** • *n* gresshoppe *f*

gray /gɹeɪ/ • *adj* grå

Greece • *n* Hellas, Grekenland **~k** • *adj* gresk; gresk, hellenesk

green /gɹiːn, gɹin/ • *adj* grønn

greeting /ˈgɹiːtɪŋ/ • *n* hilsen

grew (*sp*) ▷ GROW

grid /gɹɪd/ • *n* rutenett *n*

grief /gɹiːf/ • *n* sorg

grind /gɹaɪnd/ • *v* (*sp* ground, *pp* ground) raspe, rive, male, kverne; skrape

grocery /ˈgɹəʊsəɹi, ˈgɹoʊs(ə)ɹi/ • *n* dagligvarebutikk *m*, storsenter, landhandel *m*

gross /gɹəʊs, gɹoʊs/ • *adj* ekkel

grotesque /gɹəʊˈtɛsk, gɹoʊˈtɛsk/ • *adj* grotesk

ground /gɹaʊnd/ • *n* bakke • (*also*) ▷ GRIND

grow /gɹəʊ, gɹoʊ/ • *v* (*sp* grew, *pp* grown) vokse; dyrke **~ up** • *v* vokse opp, bli voksen **~th**; vekst

grown (*pp*) ▷ GROW

gruesome • *adj* grusom

grumpy /ˈgɹʌmpi/ • *adj* gretten

guarantee /ˌgærənˈtiː/ ; garanti *m*; garantist *m* • *v* garantere; kausjonere
guard /gɑːd, gɑɹd/ • *v* bevokte
guess /gɛs/ • *n* gjetning *f* • *v* gjette, gissa
~eline • *n* retningslinje
guinea pig /ˈgɪni pɪg/ ; prøvekanin *m*, forsøkskanin *m*
gun /gʌn/ ; skyts
~nastics • *n* gymnastikk

habit /ˈhæbɪt, ˈhæbət/ • *n* vane *m*, sedvane
had *(sp/pp)* ▷ HAVE
hail /heɪl/ • *n* hagl *n* • *v* hagle
Haiti • *n* Haiti
~ time • *n* pause *m*
halt /hɔːlt, hɑlt/ • *v* stoppe, bremse; nøle, avvente
halves *(pl)* ▷ HALF
hand /hænd/ ; handskrift, håndskrift *m* • *v* overrekke, gi
handl|e /ˈhæn.dl/ ; klinke • *v* klare
handsome /ˈhæn.səm/ • *adj* kjekk
hang| up • *v* la på røret, legge på **~over** • *n* fyllesyke *m*, bakrus *m*
happen /ˈhæpən/ • *v* foregå, inntreffe, skje
happ|y /ˈhæpiː, ˈhæpi/ • *adj* glad, lykkelig; heldig **~iness** • *n* lykke *m*, glede *m*; hell *n*

hard /hɑːd, hɑɹd/ • *adj* hard
hardware /ˈhɑːdˌwɛə, ˈhɑɹdˌwɛɹ/ ; maskinvare *m*
harm|ful /ˈhɑːmfl, ˈhɑːmfl/ • *adj* skadelig
harmon|y /ˈhɑːməni, ˈhɑːməni/ • *n* harmoni *m* **~ica** • *n* munnspill, munnharmonika
harvest /ˈhɑːvəst, ˈhɑːvɪst/ • *n* høsting *m*; avling *m* • *v* høste
hat /hæt/ • *n* hatt *m*, lue
hat|e /heɪt/ • *v* hate **~red** • *n* hat *n*
have /hæv, həv/ • *v* *(sp* had, *pp* had) ha; har hat **~ to** • *v* må
he /hiː, hi/ • *det* han
head /hɛd/ • *adj* hode-; hoved-; leder-, første • *n* hode *n*; leder *m*, sjef *m*; rektor *m*; skum *n*; evne *m*; topp *m* **~line** • *n* overskrift *f*
heal /hiːl/ • *v* hele, kurere; bli frisk
hear /hɪə(ɹ), hɪɹ/ • *v* *(sp* heard, *pp* heard) høre **~ing** • høring *f*
heard *(sp/pp)* ▷ HEAR
heat /hiːt/ • *n* varme *m*; brunst *m*; hetetokt *m* • *v* varme opp; opphisse, tenne
heaven /ˈhɛvən/ • *n* himmel *m*, sky *f*; paradis *n*
heel /hiːl/ ; skalk *m*
heir /ɛəɹ/ • *n* arving *m*
held *(sp/pp)* ▷ HOLD
hell /hɛl/ • *interj* helvete! • *n* helvete *n*
hello /həˈləʊ, hɛˈloʊ/ • *interj* hallo, hei, god dag, halla, heisann
helmet /ˈhɛlmɪt/ • *n* hjelm *m*
help /hɛlp/ • *interj* hjelp • *n* hjelp *f*; hushjelp *f* • *v* bidra til,

hjelpe til med; hjelpe til, hjelpe; hjelpe for **~ful** ● *adj* hjelpsom

hence /ˈhɛns/ ; herav, av dette følger, derfor, derav

her /hɜː(ɹ), ˈhɜˈ/ ● *det* henne, hennes, sin

herb /hɜːb, (h)ɜːb/ ; gress *n*

here /hɪə(ɹ), hɪɹ/ ● *adv* her; hit

heritage ● *n* arv

hero /ˈhɪɹoʊ, ˈhɪəɹoʊ/ ; helt *m* **~in** ● *n* heroin *m*

hesita|te /ˈhɛzɪteɪt/ ● *v* nøle med å

hid *(sp)* ▷ HIDE

hide /haɪd/ ; gjemme seg

high /haɪ/ ● *adj* høy **~light** ● *v* utheve, betone; markere **~way** ● *n* motorvei, motorveg

hike /haɪk/ ● *n* vandring *f*

hill /hɪl/ ● *n* ås *m*

hint /hɪnt/ ● *v* antyde, hinte

hire /haɪə, haɪɹ/ ● *v* ansette

his /hɪz, ˈhəz/ ● *det* hans, sin

hiss /hɪs/ ● *n* hvese

histor|y /ˈhɪst(ə)ɹi/ ● *n* historie *f*

hit /hɪt/ ● *adj* skudd *n*; slag *n*; hit *m*, slager *m*; anslag *n* ● *v (sp* hit, *pp* hit) slå; treffe; hit; ramme

hog /hɒg, hɑg/ ● *n* svin *n*

hold /həʊld, hoʊld/ ● *v (sp* held, *pp* held) holde

hole /həʊl, hoʊl/ ● *n* hull *n*; hol *n*

home /(h)əʊm, hoʊm/ ● *n* barndomshjem; hjemme; hjem *n*, heim *n*; hjemland **~work** ● *n* lekse *f*, hjemmelekse *f* **at ~** ● *phr* drive; husvarm

Honduras ● *n* Honduras

~ bee ● *n* honningbie **~moon** ● *n* hvetebrødsdager

honour *(British)* ▷ HONOR

hook /hʊk, huːk/ ● *v* huke, kroke; skru

hooves *(pl)* ▷ HOOF

hope /həʊp, hoʊp/ ● *v* håpe

horizon /həˈɹaɪzən/ ● *n* horisont *m*, blåne

horror /ˈhɔɹə, ˈhɑɹəˈ/ ● *n* gru, redsel

horse /hɔːs, hɔɹs/ ● *n* hest *m*; kavallerist *n*; bukk *m*; springer *m*

hospita|ble /hɒsˈpɪtəbəl/ ● *adj* gjestfri

hospital /ˈhɒs.pɪ.tl̩, ˈɒs.pɪ.tl̩/ ● *n* sykehus *n*

hostage /ˈhɒstɪdʒ/ ● *n* gissel *n*

hot /hɒt, hɑt/ ● *adj* varm, het; varmt, hett; sterk; heit, lekker, sexy; tampen brenner

hour /ˈaʊə(ɹ), ˈaʊəˈ/ ● *n* time

house /haʊs, hʌʊs/ ; hus *n*

how /haʊ, hæʊ/ ; hvordan ● *conj* hvordan

however /haʊˈɛvə, haʊˈɛvəˈ/ ● *adv* men, imidlertid, ikke desto mindre

howl /haʊl/ ● *v* hyle

hug /hʌg/ ● *n* klem *m* ● *v* klemme, omfavne

huh /hʌ, hə/ ● *interj* hva; eller hva

human /ˈ(h)juːmən, ˈ(h)jumən/ ● *adj* menneskelig; menneskeaktig

humble /ˈhʌmbəl, ˈʌmbəl/ ● *adj* beskjeden; ydmyk

humo|ur /hjuː.məˈ(ɹ), ˈhjuːməˈ/ ; humør *n*

hundred /ˈhʌndɹəd, ˈhʌndərd/ •
num hundre

Hungar|y • *n* Ungarn

hunger /ˈhʌŋgə, ˈhʌŋgə/ ; hungre

hunt /hʌnt/ • *n* jakt *f* • *v* jakte;
søke

hurry /ˈhʌ.ɹi, r/ • *n* travelhet *f*;
press **~ up** • *v* skynde seg

hurt /hɜːt, hɪt/ • *adj* skadet • *v*
(*sp* hurt, *pp* hurt) gjøre vont;
skade

husband /ˈhʌzbənd/ • *n*
ektemann, husbond • *v*
bevare

hyena /haɪˈiːnə/ • *n* hyene *m*

I

ic|e /aɪs, ʌɪs/ ; is *m* • *v* ise; fryse;
islegge **~y** • *adj* isete;
isbelagt, islagt; isnende

idea /aɪˈdɹə, aɪˈdi.ə/ • *n* idé *m*

Idiot /ˈɪd.i.(j)ɪt/ • *n* idiot *m*

if /ɪf/ • *conj* hvis, om, når

ignor|e /ɪgˈnɔː, ɪgˈnɔɹ/ • *v*
ignorere, overse

ill /ɪl/ • *adj* syk; kvalm
~ion • *n* illustrasjon *m*
~tion • *n* fantasi *m*, innbilning

impact /ˈɪmpækt, ɪmˈpækt/ • *n*
treffvirkning; virkning

impartial /ɪmˈpɑɹ.ʃəl/ • *adj*
upartisk, objektiv
~ation • *n* iverksetting

imply /ɪmˈplaɪ/ • *v* implisere,
medføre; insinuere

important /ɪmˈpɔːtənt, ɪmˈpɔɹtənt/
• *adj* alvorlig, betydelig, viktig

imposition /ɪm.pəˈzɪʃən/ • *n*
byrde

impress /ɪmˈpɹɛs, ˈɪmpɹɛs/ • *v*
imponere **~ive** • *adj*
imponerende

imprison /ɪmˈpɹɪzən/ • *v* fengsle

improve /ɪmˈpɹuːv/ • *v* forbedre;
forbedre seg

in /ɪn, ən/ • *adv* inne; inn; i **~ turn**
• *phr* deretter; i tur

inappropriate /ˌɪnəˈpɹəʊpɹɪ.ət,
ˌɪnəˈpɹoʊpɹɪ.ət/ • *adj*
upassende, uheldig,
malplassert, uskikket

inch /ɪntʃ/ • *n* tomme *m*

inclination /ɪn.klɪˈneɪ.ʃən/ • *n*
tilbøyelighet

income /ˈɪn.kʌm/ • *n* inntekt *f*

increas|e /ɪnˈkɹiːs, ˈɪnkɹiːs/ • *v* øke

indefatigable /ˌɪndɪˈfætɪgəbl,
ˌɪndəˈfætəgəbəl/ • *adj* utrøttelig

index /ˈɪndɛks/ • *n* (*pl* indices)
innhold *m*, indeks *m*,
innholdsfortegnelse *m*,
stikkordregister *n*

India • *n* India

indicat|e /ˈɪndɪkeɪt/ • *v* anvise
~or • *n* viser *m*; måler *m*;
indikator *m*

indices (*pl*) ▷ INDEX

indictment /ɪnˈdaɪt.mənt/ • *n*
tilltale

indolent /ˈɪn.dəl.ənt/ • *adj*
arbeidsky

industr|y /ˈɪndəstɹi/ • *n*
forretningsområde *n* **~ial** •
adj industriell

infamous /ˈɪnfəməs/ • *adj*
beryktet

infant /ˈɪn.fənt/ • *n* spedbarn *n*; barn *n*, mindreårig *m*

~n • *n* infeksjon *m*

inflation /ɪnˈfleɪʃən/ • *n* oppblåsing; inflasjon

inform /ɪnˈfɔːm, ɪnˈfɔːm/ • *v* informere **~ation** • *n* informasjon *m*

inherit /ɪnˈhɛrɪt/ • *v* arve

initiat|e /ɪˈnɪʃɪeɪt/ • *v* sette i gang **~ive** • *n* initiativ

injur|e /ˈɪndʒə, ˈɪndʒə/ • *v* skade, såre **~y** • *n* skade *m*

injured *(sp/pp)* ▷ INJURE

innovat|e /ˈməveɪt/ • *v* fornye

inside /ˈɪnsaɪd/ • *adv* inne **~er** • *n* installatør *m*

instead /ɪnˈstɛd/ • *adv* isteden, i staden, i stedet

instruct|ion /ɪnˈstrʌkʃən/ • *n* veiledning

instrument /ˈɪnstrəmənt/ ; måleapparat; redskap

insult /ɪnˈsʌlt, ˈɪnsʌlt/ • *v* skjelle ut

integral /ˈɪntɪgrəl, ˈɪntəgrəl/ • *n* integral *n*

intelligen|t /ɪnˈtɛlɪdʒənt/ • *adj* intelligent

inten|d /ɪnˈtɛnd/ • *v* ha til hensikt

interaction /ˌɪntərˈækʃən/ ; interaksjon *f*, samhandling *f*

interest /ˈɪntərɪst, ˈɪntərəst/ • *n* rente *f* **~ed** • *adj* interessert

interference /ˌɪntərˈfɪːɪns, ˌɪntəˈfɪɪəns/ • *n* interferens *m*

Internet • *n* Internett **~er** • *n* tolk

interrogate • *v* avhøra

interrupt /ˌɪntəˈrʌpt, ˌɪntəˈrʌpt/ • *v* avbryte

interval /ˈɪntəvəl, ˈɪntəvəl/ • *n* intervall

intervention /ɪntəˈvɛnʃən, ɪntəˈvɛnʃən/ • *n* intervensjon *m*

interview /ˈɪntəvjuː, ˈɪntəvjuː/ • *n* intervju

intriguing /ɪnˈtriːgɪŋ/ • *adj* Forlokkende

~ion • *n* introduksjon *m*, presentasjon *m*

invent /ɪnˈvɛnt/ • *v* oppfinne

invest /ɪnˈvɛst/ • *v* investere

invisible /ɪnˈvɪzəb(ə)l/ • *adj* usynlig

Iran • *n* Iran

Ir|eland • *n* Irland

iron /ˈaɪən, ˈaɪən/ ; strykejern *n* • *v* stryke

irony /ˈaɪə.rən.i, ˈaɪ.rə.ni/ ; skjebnens ironi

irritat|e /ˈɪrɪteɪt/ • *v* irritere **~ing** • *adj* irriterende, irriterende

isolate /ˈaɪsəleɪt, ˈaɪsələt/ • *v* isolere

issue /ˈɪsjuː, ˈɪʃ(j)uː/ • *n* problem *n*

it /ɪt, ət/ • *pron* det; den **~s** • *det* dens, dets

jail /dʒeɪl/ • *n* fengsel

jam /ˈdʒæm, ˈdʒæːm/ ; trengsel; vanskelighet/ trøbbel/ knipe ´

jar /dʒɑː, dʒɑr/ • *n* krukke

jaw /dʒɔː, dʒɔ/ • *n* kjeve

jealous /ˈdʒɛləs/ ● *adj* sjalu; misunnelig

jeans /dʒiːnz/ ● *n* jeans *m*, olabukse *f*

jellyfish /ˈdʒɛliˌfɪʃ/ ● *n* manet

~ish ● *adj* jødisk

job /dʒɒb, dʒab/ ● *n* jobb *n*, arbeid *n*

join /dʒɔɪn/ ● *v* sammenstille

joke /dʒəʊk, dʒoʊk/ ● *n* vits *m* ● *v* tulle, tulle bort, kødde

journal /ˈdʒɜːnəl/ ● *n* dagbok *f*; tidsskrift *n*

journalis|t /ˈdʒɜːnəlɪst, ˈdʒɜːnəlɪst/ ; journalist *m*; reporter *m* **~m** ● *n* journalistikk

journey /ˈdʒɜːni, ˈdʒɜːni/ ● *n* reise

juice /dʒuːs, dʒus/ ● *n* juice, jus

jump /dʒʌmp/ ● *n* hopp *n*, sprang *n*; skvetting *m* ● *v* hoppe; snike, gå forbi; skvette; hoppe over

jungle /ˈdʒʌŋgəl/ ● *n* jungel *m*

just /dʒʌst/ ● *adj* nettopp

K

keep /kiːp/ ● *n* borgtårn; forpleining, underhold ● *v* (*sp* kept, *pp* kept) beholde; bevare; fortsette **~er** ● *n* keeper *m*

kept *(sp/pp)* ▷ KEEP

kestrel /ˈkɛstrəl/ ● *n* falk, hauk; tårnfalk

key /kiː, ki/ ; tast *m*; nøkkel *m* **~board** ● *n* tastatur *n*; klaviatur *n*; elektronisk orgel *n*, keyboard *n*

kick /kɪk/ ; spark ● *v* sparke

kid /kɪd/ ● *n* killing *m*, kje *n*; barn *n*, unge *m*; ungdom *m* ● *v* lure; tulle; tøyse, kødde

kidnap ● *v* kidnappe

kill /kɪl/ ● *n* drap *m* ● *v* drepe **~er** ● *n* morder *m*, drapsmann *m*

kind /kaɪnd/ ● *adj* snill, vennlig ● *n* slag *n*

~dom ● *n* kongerike *n*, kongedømme *n*, kongeriket

Kiribati ● *n* Kiribati

kiss /kɪs/ ● *n* kyss *n*; pikekyss *n* ● *v* kysse

knee /niː, ni/ ● *n* kne *n*

kneel /niːl/ ● *v* (*sp* knelt, *pp* knelt) knele

kneeled *(sp/pp)* ▷ KNEEL

knelt *(sp/pp)* ▷ KNEEL

knew *(sp)* ▷ KNOW

knife /naɪf/ ; knivblad *n* **under the ~** ● *phr* under kniven

knit /nɪt/ ● *v* (*sp* knitted, *pp* knitted) strikke

knitted ▷ KNIT

knives *(pl)* ▷ KNIFE

knock /nɒk, nak/ ● *v* banke; støte, slå, dunke

know /nəʊ, noʊ/ ● *v* (*sp* knew, *pp* known) vite; kjenne; kunne; forstå

known *(pp)* ▷ KNOW

kookaburra /ˈkʊkəˌbʌrə, ˈkʊkəˌbʌrə/ ● *n* kokaburra

Kosov|o ● *n* Kosovo

Kyrgyzstan ● *n* Kirgisistan

label /ˈleɪbəl/ • *n* etikett • *v* merke

lack /lak, læk/ • *n* mangel *m* • *v* mangle

lad /læd, ləd/ • *n* ladd *m*

lady /ˈleɪdɪ/ • *n* dame

laid *(sp/pp)* ▷ LAY

lain *(pp)* ▷ LIE

lamb /læm/ • *n* lam *n*

lamp /læmp/ • *n* lampe *f* **~post** • *n* lyktestolpe

land /lænd/ • *n* land *n* • *v* lande

language /ˈlæŋɡwɪdʒ, æ/ ; språk *n*, programmeringsspråk *n*

Laos • *n* Laos

lap /læp/ • *n* fang *n*

large /lɑːdʒ, lɑɪdʒ/ • *adj* stor

laser /ˈleɪz.ə(ɹ), ˈleɪzɚ/ • *n* laser *m*

last /lɑːst, læst/ • *adj* sist, senest; nyest • *adv* sist

late /leɪt/ • *adj* sein; som har gått bort, som har gått fra oss **~r** • *adv* senere

Latin • *n* latin latinsk

latter /ˈlæt.ə(ɹ), ˈlæt̬.ɚ/ ; sist

laugh /lɑːf, lɑːf/ • *n* latter *m*, lått *m*; vits *m* • *v* le, skratte **~ter** • *n* latter

laundry /ˈlɔːn.dɹi, ˈlɑn.dɹi/ • *n* klesvask *m*; vaskerom *n*; skittentøy *n*

law /lɔː, lɒ/ • *n* lov *m*; loven

lay /leɪ/ • *v* (*sp* laid, *pp* laid) legge; dekke • *(also)* ▷ LIE

lead /lɛd/ • *n* bly • *v* (*sp* led, *pp* led) føre **~er** • *n* leder *m*, fører *m*

leaf /liːf/ • *n* blad *n*; folie *m*; ark *n*; løv

leak /liːk/ • *n* lekkasje *m* • *v* lekke

lean /liːn/ • *adj* slank; mager

leaned *(sp/pp)* ▷ LEAN

leant *(sp/pp)* ▷ LEAN

leap /liːp/ • *v* (*sp* leapt, *pp* leapt) sprang, hopp, hoppe

leaped *(sp/pp)* ▷ LEAP

leapt *(sp/pp)* ▷ LEAP

learn /lɜːn, lɜn/ • *v* (*sp* learnt, *pp* learnt) lære

learned *(sp/pp)* ▷ LEARN

learnt *(sp/pp)* ▷ LEARN

leave /liːv/ • *n* løyve • *v* (*sp* left, *pp* left) etterlate; forlate

leaves *(pl)* ▷ LEAF

led *(sp/pp)* ▷ LEAD

left /lɛft/ • *adj* venstre • *n* venstresiden • *(also)* ▷ LEAVE

leg /lɛɡ, leɪɡ/ • *n* bein *n*; etappe *m*; spill *n*, kamp *m*, parti *n*; side, sidekant *m*

legacy /ˈlɛɡəsi, ˈleɪɡəsi/ ; foreldet; arv *m*

legislati|ve /ˈlɛ.dʒɪ.slə.tɪv, ˈlɛ.dʒɪ.sleɪ.tɪv/ • *adj* legislativ

lend /lɛnd/ • *v* (*sp* lent, *pp* lent) låne

lens /lɛnz/ ; linse *f*

lent *(sp/pp)* ▷ LEND

lesbian /ˈlɛzbi.ən/ • *adj* lesbe • *n* lesbe *f*

Lesotho • *n* Lesotho

less /lɛs/ • *adj* mindre; færre • *adv* mindre • *prep* minus, fratrukket

let /lɛt/ • v (sp let, pp let) la; leie ut

level /ˈlɛv.əl/ • adj vatret • n vater n; nivå n • v gå videre til neste nivå

liberate /ˈlɪbəɹeɪt/ • v frigjøre

Liberia • n Liberia

library /ˈlaɪbɹəɹi, ˈlaɪbɹɛɪi/ • n bibliotek n **~ian** • n bibliotekar m

Libya • n Libya

lice (pl) ▷ LOUSE

licence (British) ▷ LICENSE

lid /lɪd/ • n lokk

lie /laɪ/ • n leie n; løgn m • v (sp lay, pp lain) ligge; lyve, ljuge

life /laɪf/ ; liv n; livstid m; levetid f **~style** • n livsstil m

lift /lɪft/ ; løft n • v løfte, heve; loppe

light /laɪt, lʌɪt/ • adj lett; lyst, opplyst, belyst; lys, blek; banal, enkel • n lys; flamme • v (sp lit, pp lit) opplyse; tenne; losse **~ning** • n lyn, lynglimt, blink

lighted (sp/pp) ▷ LIGHT

like /laɪk/ • prep lik, som • v like, synes om **~wise**; i like måte

likely /ˈlaɪkli/ • adj sannsynlig

limit /ˈlɪmɪt/ • n begrensning

line /laɪn/ • n linje f **~ar** • adj lineær

lion /ˈlaɪən/ ; løve

lip /lɪp/ • n leppe

liquid /ˈlɪkwɪd/ • adj flytende; likvid

Lisbon • n Lisboa, Lissabon

listen /ˈlɪs.ən/ • v lytte; lystre; høre

lit (sp/pp) ▷ LIGHT

literary /ˈlɪtəɹəɹi, ˈlɪtəɹɛ(ə)ɹi/ ; :

Lithuania • n Litauen

little /ˈlɪtəl, ˈlɪtl̩/ • adj liten; lille-

live /lɪv/ • adv direkte, live • v leve; bo

lives (pl) ▷ LIFE

load /loʊd, ləʊd/ • v laste

loan /ləʊn, loʊn/ • n lån

lobster /ˈlɒb.stə, ˈlɑb.stɚ/ • n hummer

local /ˈləʊkl̩, ˈloʊkl̩/ • adj lokal **~ize** • v lokalisere **~ization** • n lokalisering f **~er** • n skap n **~out** • v logge ut

logic /ˈlɒdʒɪk, ˈlɑdʒɪk/ • n logikk m **~al** • adj logisk

logistics • n logistikk **~iness** • n ensomhet

long /lɒŋ, lɔːŋ/ • adj lang • v lengte

look /lʊk, luːk/ ; utseende n; uttrykk n • v oppsøke; se, skue; se ut; synes; se etter, søke, leite **~ up** • v slå opp **~ down on sb** • v se ned på, rakke ned på **~ for sb/sth** • v være ute etter **~ out** • v pass opp **~ up to sb** • v se opp til

loophole /ˈluː.phəʊl/ • n skyteskår n; smutthull n

lose /luːz/ • v (sp lost, pp lost) miste

lost /lɒst, lɔːst/ • adj tapt • (also) ▷ LOSE

lot /lɒt, lɑt/ • n skjebne

love /lʌv, lɔːv/ ; elskling m, kjæreste, min elskede, kjære; null • v elske; like; elske med

low /ləʊ, loʊ/ ● *adj* lav ● *n*
lågtrykksområde *n*
~ty ● *n* lojalitet *m*
luck|y /ˈlʌki/ ● *adj* heldig
Luxembourg ● *n* Luxembourg,
Luxemburg
lyrics /ˈlɪɹɪks/ ● *n* tekst *f*

M

Macedonia ● *n* Makedonia
mad /mæd, ˈmæːd/ ● *adj* gal,
sprø; sint, sinna, olm
made *(sp/pp)* ▷ MAKE
Madrid ● *n* Madrid
magazine /mægəˈzin, mægəˈziːn/
● *n* tidsskrift, magasin
maggot /ˈmægət/ ● *n* maddik
magic /ˈmadʒɪk, ˈmædʒɪk/ ● *adj*
magisk
magnet /ˈmægnət/ ● *n* magnet *m*
~ic ● *adj* magnetisk;
fengslende, forførisk,
lokkende, tiltrekkende
magnify /ˈmagnɪfaɪ, ˈmægnɪfaɪ/ ●
v forstørre
main /meɪn/ ● *adj* hoved- **~land**
● *n* fastland *n*
maint|ain /meɪnˈteɪn/ ● *v*
opprettholde, bevare,
vedlikeholde
major /ˈmeɪdʒə(ɹ), ˈmeɪdʒɹ/ ● *adj*
myndig; dur **~ity**; majoritet *m*,
seiersmargin *m*;
myndighetsalder *m*

make /meɪk/ ● *v* (*sp* made, *pp*
made) lage; tjene **~ up**; finne
på
Malawi ● *n* Malawi
male /meɪl/ ● *adj* mannlig, hann-
mallard /ˈmæl.ɑː(ɹ)d, ˈmælərd/ ● *n*
stokkand
man /mæn/ ● *n* (*pl* man)
menneske ● *v* bemanne
manage /ˈmænɪdʒ/ ● *v* lede;
håndtere, klare **~r**; manager
m, impressario *m*
mandatory /ˈmæn.də.t(ə)ɹi,
ˈmæn.də.tɔ.ɹi/ ● *adj*
obligatorisk
manifest /ˈmæn.ɪ.fɛst/ ● *adj*
manifest, åpenbar ● *n*
manifest *n* ● *v* manifestere
manuscript /ˈmænjəˌskɹɪpt/ ● *n*
manuskript *n*
marble /ˈmɑːbəl, ˈmɑːɹbəl/ ● *n*
marmor *m*; klinkekule *f*
march /mɑːtʃ, mɑːɹtʃ/ ● *n* marsj *m*;
gang *m*, forløp *m*; grenseland
n ● *v* marsjere *m*; rykke frem
mark /mɑːk/ ● *n* merke *n*;
karakter, flekk *m*
market /ˈmɑːkɪt, ˈmɑːɹkɪt/ ● *n*
marked *n*, markedsplass *m*;
markeds-
marmot /ˈmɑːɹ.mət/ ● *n*
murmeldyr *n*
~ied ● *adj* gift
Mars ● *n* Mars
massacre /ˈmæs.ə.kəɹ,
ˈmæs.ə.kə(ɹ)/ ● *n* massakre ● *v*
massakrere
master /ˈmɑːstə, ˈmæstəɹ/ ● *adj*
hoved-; mester-; original- ● *n*
mester *m*; original *m*,
masterkopi *m*; herre *m* ● *v*

lede; styre; mestre, beherske
~piece • *n* mesterverk *n*,
mesterstykke *n*

match /mætʃ/ • *n* kamp *m*,
match *m*; like, likemann *m*,
jevnbyrdig; fyrstikk *m* • *v*
passe sammen, stemme
overens

material /məˈtɪɪɪ.əl, məˈtɪəɪɪəl/ •
adj materiell • *n* materiale *n*;
stoff; tøy *n*

mathematic|s /ˌmæθ(ə)ˈmætɪks/ •
n matematikk *m* **~al**; teoretisk

maths ▷ MATHEMATICS

mature /məˈtjʊə, məˈtʃʊ(ə)ɪ/ • *adj*
voksen, moden

may /meɪ/ • *v* (*sp* might, *pp* -)
kan, få, må; kan være, also
expressed with adv. kanskje

maybe /ˈmeɪbi/ • *adv* kanskje;
kan hende, kanskje det

me /miː, mi/ • *pron* jeg; meg; min

mean /miːn/ • *v* (*sp* meant, *pp*
meant) bety **~ing** • *n* mening,
betydning; tyding

meant (*sp/pp*) ▷ MEAN

meanwhile /ˈmiːnwaɪl, ˈmiːnhwaɪl/
; imens

measure /ˈmɛʒə, ˈmɛʒɚ/ • *n* mål *n*
~ment • *n* måling

mechani|c • *n* mekaniker *m*

medicine /ˈmɛd.sɪn, ˈmɛ.dɪ.sɪn/ ;
medisin *m*

melod|y /ˈmɛl.ə.di, ˈmɛl.ə.di/ • *n*
melodi *m*

melt /mɛlt/ • *v* (*sp* melted, *pp*
molten) smelte

melted (*sp/pp*) ▷ MELT

member /ˈmɛmbə, ˈmɛmbɚ/ ; lem
n

memor|y /ˈmɛm(ə)ɹi, ˈmɪm(ə)ɹi/ ;
dataminne *n*

men (*pl*) ▷ MAN

mention /ˈmɛnʃən/ • *n* omtale *m*
• *v* omtale

menu /ˈmɛnjuː, ˈmɛnjuː/ ; meny *m*

Mercury /ˈməː.kjʊ.ɹi, ˈmɜːkjəɹi/ • *n*
Merkur

merc|y /ˈmɜːsi, ˈmɜːsi/ • *n*
barmhjertighet, nåde

mess /mɛs/ • *n* røre

met (*sp/pp*) ▷ MEET

metal /ˈmɛtəl/ ; metal

meteorite /ˈmiː.tɪ.ə.ɹaɪt,
ˈmiː.ti.ə.ɹaɪt/ • *n* meteoritt *m*

~ist • *n* meteorolog *m*

meticulous /mɪˈtɪkjɪlɪs/ • *adj*
omhyggelig

metre (*British*) ▷ METER

metropolitan /ˌmɛtɹəˈpɒlɪtən,
ˌmɛtɹəˈpɑlɪtən/ • *adj*
metropolitt • *n* byregion

Mexic|o • *n* Mexico

mice (*pl*) ▷ MOUSE

Micronesia ;
Mikronesiaføderasjonen

middle /ˈmɪdəl, ˈmədəl/ • *adj*
midterst **~ name** • *n*
mellomnavn *n*

midwife /ˈmɪd.waɪf/ ;
fødselshjelper *m*

mighty /ˈmaɪti/ • *adj* mektig

military /ˈmɪl.ɪ.tɹi, ˈmɪl.ɪ.tɛɹi/ • *adj*
militær

mill /mɪl/ ; mølle *m*, fabrikk *m*

million /ˈmɪljən/ • *num* million *m*

mind /maɪnd/ • *n* forstand *m*,
intellekt *n*; bevissthet *m*;
hukommelse *m*, minne *n*;
konsentrasjon *m*; tenker *m*;
innstilling *m*; hensikt *m*,

intensjon *m*; ånd *m* • *v* huske, passe på; bry seg om, ha imot, ha noe imot, bry

mine /maɪn/ ; mine *f* • *pron* min *m* • *v* minelegge

mineral /ˈmɪ.nə.ɹ.əl/ ; mineral *m*; mineralvann *n*

~ry; Kabinett

minute /ˈmɪnɪt/ • *n* minutt *n*; øyeblikk *n*; protokoll *m*

misbehavior /ˌmɪsbəˈheɪvjɚ, ˌmɪsbəˈheɪvjə/ • *n* dårlig oppførsel *m*

miss /mɪs/ • *n* frøken • *v* savne

missile /ˈmɪsaɪl/ • *n* missil

mission /ˈmɪʃ(ə)n/ • *n* misjon *m* **~ary** • *n* misjonær *m*

mistake /mɪˈsteɪk/ • *n* feilgrep *n* • *v* misforstå; ta feil

mix /mɪks/ • *v* blande, mikse

mobile /ˈməʊbaɪl, ˈmoʊbəl/ • *adj* bevegelig, mobil • *n* uro *m*

mode /məʊd, moʊd/ ; mote

modern /ˈmɒd(ə)n, ˈmɑdɚn/ • *adj* moderne

Moldova • *n* Moldova

mole /məʊl, moʊl/ • *n* føflekk *m*

molecul|e /ˈmɒləkjuːl, ˈmɑləkjul/ • *n* molekyl *n*

molten *(pp)* ▷ MELT

moment /ˈməʊmənt, ˈmoʊmənt/ ; moment *n* **at the ~** • *phr* i øyeblikket, akkurat nå

Monaco • *n* Monaco

Monday • *adv* på mandag • *n* mandag

money /ˈmʌni/ ; kontanter **~ laundering** • *n* hvitvasking *m*

Mongolia • *n* Mongolia

monitor /ˈmɒnɪtə/ • *v* overvåke

monk /mʌŋk/ • *n* munk *m*

monster /ˈmɒnstə(ɹ), ˈmɑnstɚ/ • *n* monster *n*

month /mʌnθ/ • *n* måned

mood /muːd/ • *n* humør *n*; dårlig humør; stemning *f*

moon /muːn/ • *n* månen *m*; måne *m* **over the ~** • *phr* overlykkelig

moose /muːs/ • *n* elg *m*

morbid /ˈmɔː.bɪd, ˈmɔɪ.bɪd/ • *adj* morbid

mortgage /ˈmɔː.ɡɪdʒ, ˈmɔɪ.ɡɪdʒ/ • *n* hypothek *n*

most /məʊst, moʊst/ ; høyst, meget, veldig

mount /maʊnt/ • *v* bestige; montere

mouse /maʊs, mʌʊs/ • *n* (*pl* mice) mus *f*; datamus *f*

mouth /maʊθ, mʌʊθ/ • *n* munn *m*, kjeft **~ful** • *n* munnfull *m*

move /muːv/ ; trekk *n* • *v* handle; flytte; røre **~ment**; bevegelse

mow /məʊ, moʊ/ • *v* (*sp* mowed, *pp* mown) slå, skjære, klippe

mowed *(sp/pp)* ▷ MOW

mown *(pp)* ▷ MOW

Mr. • *n* herr

Mrs • *n* fru, Fr

much /mʌtʃ/ • *det* mye

mud /mʌd/ • *n* søle *f*, gjørme *f*, leire *f*

municipal /mjuˈnɪsɪpəl/ • *adj* kommunal, kommune-

murder /ˈmɜːdə(ɹ), ˈmɜ.dɚ/ • *n* mord *n*; overlagt drap • *v* myrde; ta knekken på; drepe **~** • *n* mord *n*; overlagt drap • *v* myrde; ta knekken på; drepe

musc|le /ˈmʌs.əl/ • *n* muskel

M

museum /mjuˈziːəm, mjuˈziˌəm/ • *n* museum

music /ˈmjuːzɪk, ˈmjuzɪk/ • *n* musikk *m*; noter

must /mʌst, məs(t)/ • *n* krav *n*, must *m* • *v* måtte

mute /mjuːt/ • *adj* stum • *n* sordin *m*; skitt *m*, dritt *m* • *v* slå av, dempe

mutual /ˈmjuːtʃuəl/ • *adj* gjensidig; felles

my /maɪ, mɪ/ • *det* min *m*

Myanmar • *n* Myanmar, Burma

myself /maɪˈsɛlf/ • *pron* meg selv

myster|y /ˈmɪstəɹi/ • *n* mysterium *n* **~ious** • *adj* mystiskt

N

nail /neɪl/ ; spiker *m* • *v* spikre; fange, fakke; treffe

naked /ˈneɪkɪd, ˈnɛkɪd/ • *adj* naken

name /neɪm/ • *n* navn; ry *n* • *v* kalle, navngi; velge; nevne; utnevne

~-minded • *adj* bornert, innskrenket, trangsynt

nation /ˈneɪʃən/ • *n* nasjon *m*

NATO • *n* (*abbr* North Atlantic Treaty Organization) NATO

natur|e /ˈneɪtʃə, ˈneɪtʃɚ/ • *n* natur *m*

naughty /ˈnɔːti, ˈnɔti/ • *adj* uskikkelig; frekk, uforskamma

navigat|e /ˈnæv.ɪ.ɡeɪt/ • *v* navigere

~ily • *adv* nødvendigvis

neck /nɛk/ ; hals *m*

need /niːd/ • *v* trenge

negative /ˈnɛɡətɪv, ˈnɛ(e)ɡəˌɹɪv/ • *adj* negativ

negotiat|e /nəˈɡəʊˌʃiˌeɪt, nəˈɡoʊˌʃiˌeɪt/ • *v* forhandle; drøfte **~ion** • *n* forhandling

neighbo|ur /ˈneɪbə, ˈneɪbɚ/ • *n* nabo *m* **~rhood** • *n* naboskap *n*; strøk; naboer; boområder

neighbourhood (*British*) ▷ NEIGHBORHOOD

neither /ˈnaɪð.ə(ɹ), ˈnaɪðɚ/ ; ei heller • *det* ingen av

Neptune • *n* Neptun

net /nɛt/ ; nett **~work** • *n* nett *n*; nettverk *n*

Netherlands • *adj* nederlandsk • *n* Nederland, Holland

never /ˈnɛv.ə(ɹ), ˈnɛ.vɚ/ • *adv* aldri

new /njuː, n(j)u/ • *adj* ny; nåværende; nyfødt **~lywed** • *adj* nygift

~paper • *n* avispapir *n*

next /nɛkst/ • *adj* neste; nærmest; følgende • *adv* nærmest; som neste • *n* neste *m*, nestemann *m* • *prep* ved siden av, attmed **~ to** • *prep* ved siden av, hos

nice /naɪs/ • *adj* hyggelig, sympatisk; pen; fin

Nigeria • *n* Nigeria

night /naɪt/ • *n* natt *m*; aften *m*; overnatting *m*; nattesøvn *m*; skumring *m*; mørke *m* **~mare** • *n* mareritt *n* **~stand** • *n* nattbord *n*

nightingale /ˈnaɪtɪŋɡeɪl/ • *n*
sørnattergal

nin|e /naɪn/ • *num* ni **~eteen** •
num nitten **~ety** • *num* nitti

no • *det* ingen; forbudt • *n* nei *n*
• *part* ingen; forbudt ~ **one** •
pron ingen

noble /ˈnəʊbəl, ˈnoʊbəl/ • *adj* edel

nod /nɒd, nɑd/ • *n* nikk *n* • *v*
nikke

noon /nuːn/ • *n* non *m*

nor /nɔː, nɔːr/ • *conj* eller, heller
ikke

norm /nɔːm/ • *n* norm

normal /ˈnɔːməl, ˈnɔːrməl/ • *adj*
normal, ordinær, vanlig,
alminnelig **~ity** • *n* normalitet
m

north /nɔːθ, nɔːrθ/ • *n* nord
~book • *n* skrivebok

nothing /ˈnʌθɪŋ/ ; ingenting
~ness • *n* ingenting

notice /ˈnəʊtɪs, ˈnoʊtɪs/ • *v*
bemerke

notify /ˈnəʊtɪfaɪ/ • *v* meddele

noun /naʊn, næːn/ ; nomen *n*

nourishment • *n* ernæring *f*

novice /ˈnɒvɪs/ • *n* nybegynner
m, novise *m*

now /naʊ/ • *conj* nå som
~ar • *adj* nukleær;
kjerne-/atom-,
kjernekraft/atomkraft

number /ˈnʌmbə, ˈnʌmbər/ ;
numerus *m*

nut /nʌt/ ; mutter *m*; galning *m*,
gærning *m*; ball *m*

nutritio|n /njuːˈtrɪʃən, nuˈtrɪʃən/ •
n ernæring **~us** • *adj*
næringsrik

oak /oʊk, əʊk/ ; eik *f*

obes|e /oʊˈbiːs, əʊˈbiːs/ • *adj*
korpulent **~ity** • *n* fedme

obe|y /oʊˈbeɪ, əʊˈbeɪ/ • *v* adlyde;
være lydhør **~dience** • *n*
lydighet

object /ˈɒb.dʒɛkt, ˈɑb.dʒɛkt/ • *n*
objekt *n*, ting *m*, gjenstand *m*
~ion • *n* protest *m*, innvending
f

obnoxious /əbˈnɒkʃəs, əbˈnɑkʃəs/
• *adj* ufyselig, utålelig

obvious /ˈɑ(b).vi.əs, ˈɒ(b).vɪəs/ •
adj opplagt, innlysende **~ly** •
adv selvsagt, åpenbart

~ally • *adv* sporadisk, av og til,
nå og da

occup|y /ˈɒkjʊpaɪ, ˈɑkjəpaɪ/ • *v*
besette **~ation** • *n* yrke *n*;
okkupasjon *m*

occur /əˈkɜː, əˈkɜ/ • *v* skje;
inntreffe **~rence** • *n* tilfelle *n*

odd /ɒd, ɑd/ • *adj* ulike

of /ɒv, ɔv/ • *prep* av

off /ɒf, ɔːf/ • *adj* av, deaktivert

offer /ˈɒfə(r), ˈɔfər/ • *n* forslag *n* •
v foreslå; tilby

office /ˈɒfɪs, ˈɔfɪs/ • *n* kontor *n*

official /əˈfɪʃəl/ • *adj* offisiell

often /ˈɒf(t)ən, ˈɔf(t)ən/ • *adv* ofte,
hyppig

oh /əʊ, oʊ/ • *interj* oi, å, ai

oil /ɔɪl/ • *n* matolje, olje *m*;
petroleum *m* • *v* olje; smøre

OK • *n* alt i orden

old /əʊld, ˈoʊld/ ; gammel

on /ɒn, ɑn/ ; på
once /wʌn(t)s, wʌns/ ● *conj* så
snart, med det første **~ again**
● *adv* en gang til
onion /ˈʌnjən, ˈʌnjɪn/ ● *n* løk *m*
only /ˈəʊn.li, ˈəʊn.lɪ/ ● *adv* bare
open /ˈəʊ.pən, ˈoʊ.pən/ ● *v* åpne,
lukke opp; ta opp; innlede;
åpnes
opera /ˈɒp.ə.ɹə, ˈɑ.pɹɑ.ə/ ● *n* opera
~on ● *n* operasjon *m*
opinion /əˈpɪnjən/ ● *n* mening,
synspunkt *n*
opposit|e /ˈɒpəzɪt, ˈɑp(ə)sɪt/ ● *adj*
motsatt ● *n* motsatt
optimis|tic /ˌɒptɪˈmɪstɪk,
ˌɑptɪˈmɪstɪk/ ● *adj* optimistisk
~m ● *n* optimisme *m*
option /ˈɒpʃən, ˈɑpʃən/ ● *n*
valgmulighet *m*
or /ɔː(ɹ), ɔɹ/ ● *conj* eller
orange /ˈɒɹɪn(d)ʒ, ˈɑɹɪndʒ/ ● *adj*
oransje ● *n* appelsintre *n*;
appelsin *m*; oransje *m*
order /ˈɔː.də, ˈɔɹdɹ/ ● *n* ordning *m*,
orden *m*, rekkefølge *m*; ordre
m ● *v* ordne; bestille
oregano /ɒɹɪˈɡɑːnəʊ, ɔˈɹɛɡənoʊ/ ●
n kung, bergmynte
origin /ˈɒɹɪdʒɪn, ˈɔɹɪdʒɪn/ ; origo
Oslo ● *n* Oslo
other /ˈʌðə(ɹ), ʊðɹ/ ● *adj* annen,
andre
our /ˈaʊə(ɹ), ˈaʊɹ/ ● *det* vår
out /aʊt, æɛt/ ● *adv* ut; ute, borte;
vekk; av ● *prep* ut av **~ing** ● *n*
oute **~rageous** ● *adj* uhørt
~side ● *n* ytterside ● *prep*
utside **~standing** ● *adj*
fremragende; utstående; **~ of the blue** ●

phr ut av det blå, som lyn fra
klar himmel
over /ˈəʊ.və(ɹ), ˈoʊ.və/ ● *adj* over,
slutt **~all** ● *n* overall *m* **~react**
● *v* overreagere
owe /əʊ, oʊ/ ● *v* skylde
own /ˈəʊn, ˈoʊn/ ● *v* eie

pace /peɪs/ ; pass
~et ● *n* pakke *m*
pad /pæd/ ● *n* pute *f*; blokk *f*;
hjem *n*
paid *(sp/pp)* ▷ PAY
pain /peɪn/ ; pine
paint /peɪnt/ ● *n* maling, lakk ● *v*
male, lakkere **~ing**; maleri
pale /peɪl/ ● *adj* blek, bleik ● *n*
påle *m*, pæl *m*; stolpe ● *v*
blekne
pan /pæn/ ● *n* panne ● *v* slakte;
panorere
Panama ● *n* Panama
panda /ˈpandə, ˈpændə/ ● *n* panda
m, pandabjørn, kjempepanda
panic /ˈpænɪk/ ● *n* panikk *m* ● *v*
få panikk
pants /pænts/ ● *n* bukse *f*, brok
paper /ˈpeɪpə, ˈpeɪpɹ/ ● *adj* papir
● *n* ark; artikkel *m*
paragraph /ˈpɛɹəɡɹæf, ˈpæɹəɡɹɑːf/
● *n* avsnitt
parallel /ˈpæɹəˌlɛl, ˈpɛɹəˌlɛl/ ● *adj*
parallell ● *adv* parallelt ● *n*
parallell *m*

parliament /ˈpɑːləmənt, ˈpɑːləmənt/ ● *n* ting, parlament

parrot /ˈpærət/ ● *n* papegøye *m*

part /pɑːt, pɑːt/ ● *n* del *m*; rolle *m* ● *v* forlate, dra; dele

participa|te /pɑːˈtɪsɪpeɪt/ ● *v* delta

particle /ˈpɑːtɪk(ə)l, ˈpɑːtɪkəl/ ● *n* partikkel *m*

particular /pəˈtɪkjələ, pəˈtɪkjələ/ ● *adj* bestemt

pass /pɑːs, pæs/ ● *v* passere ~ **away** ● *v* gå bort

passive /ˈpæsɪv/ ● *adj* passiv ~**ly** ● *adv* passivt

past /pɑːst, pæst/ ● *n* fortid; preteritum ● *prep* forbi, bortenfor

pasta /ˈpæstə, ˈpɑːstə/ ● *n* pasta

patien|t /ˈpeɪʃ(ə)nt, ˈpeɪʃənt/ ● *n* pasient *m* ~**ce**; kabal

pause /pɔːz, pɒz/ ● *n* pause *f*

PC *(abbr)* ▷ COMPUTER

pea /piː/ ● *n* ert

peanut /ˈpiːnʌt, ˈpiːnət/ ● *n* peanøtt *f*, jordnøtt *f*

~ crossing ● *n* sebrastripe

peel /piːl/ ● *n* skall *n* ● *v* skrelle

pelican /ˈpɛlɪkən/ ● *n* pelikan *m*

pen /pɛn, pɪn/ ● *n* innhegning *f*, kve *n* ● *v* (*sp* pent, *pp* pent) innhegne; skrive, føre i pennen

penalty ● *n* straff *f*

pencil /ˈpɛnsəl, ˈpɛnsɪl/ ● *n* blyant

pendulum /ˈpɛndʒələm, ˈpɪndʒələm/ ● *n* pendel *m*

penetrate /ˈpɛnɪtreɪt, ˈpɛnɪˌtreɪt/ ● *v* trenge inn

penguin /ˈpɛŋgwɪn, ˈpɪŋgwɪn/ ● *n* pingvin *m*

penned *(sp/pp)* ▷ PEN

pension /ˈpɛnʃ(ə)n/ ● *n* pensjon *m*; pensjonat *n*

pensive /ˈpɛn.sɪv/ ● *adj* tankefull, ettertenksom

pent *(sp/pp)* ▷ PEN

people /ˈpiːpəl, ˈpiːpəl/ ● *n* folk, lyd *m*; slekt *m*

pepper /ˈpɛpə, ˈpɛpə/ ● *n* pepper *n*

perfect /ˈpɜː.fɪkt, ˈpɜːfɪkt/ ● *adj* perfekt ~**ly** ● *adv* perfekt

perhaps /pəˈhæps, pəˈhæps/ ● *adv* kanskje, muligens

period /ˈpɪərɪəd/ ● *n* periode, æra; punktum *n*

~**ly** ● *adv* permanent, for alltid

~**ssion** ● *n* tillatelse *m*

Persian ● *adj* persisk

personnel /pɜː.səˈnɛl, pɜː.səˈnɛl/ ● *n* personell

persuade /pəˈsweɪd, pəˈsweɪd/ ● *v* overtale

Peru ● *n* Peru

pet /pɛt/ ● *v* kjæle; kose med, kjærtegne

photo ▷ PHOTOGRAPH

photograph /ˈfəʊtəˌɡrɑːf, ˈfəʊtəˌɡrɑːf/ ● *v* fotografere ~**y** ● *n* fotografi

physical /ˈfɪzɪkəl/ ● *adj* fysisk

pian|o /pɪˈænəʊ, pɪˈænəʊ/ ● *n* piano *n*

pick /pɪk/ ● *n* hakke; dirk *m*; valg *n* ● *v* pilke; plukke; velge

picky /ˈpɪki/ ● *adj* pirkete

picture /ˈpɪktʃə, ˈpɪk(t)ʃə/ ● *n* bilde *n*; kino *m* ● *v* fotografere; forestille seg

pig /pɪg/ ● *n* svin *n*, gris *m*; storeter *m*; purk *m*, snut *m*

pike /paɪk/ ● *n* pik *m*; gjedde *f*

pile /paɪl/ • *n* haug *m*, stabel *m*; batteri *n*

pillow /ˈpɪləʊ/ • *n* pute

pin /pɪn/ • *n* knappenål

piranha /pɪˈrɑːnjə, pɪˈrɑnjə/ • *n* piraya

pira|te /ˈpaɪ(ə)rɪt/ • *adj* piratkopiert • *n* pirat *m* • *v* piratkopiere **~cy** • *n* kapring

pitch /pɪtʃ/ • *n* bek *n*

place /pleɪs/ • *n* sted *n*; plass *m*; ståsted *n*; rolle *m*; posisjon *m* • *v* plassere; plassere seg; treffe; sette **~holder** • *n* plassholder *m*

plan /plæn/ • *v* planlegge

plane /pleɪn/ • *adj* plan • *n* plan *n*; høvel *m*; fly *n* • *v* plane; høvle

plastic /ˈplɑːstɪk, ˈplæstɪk/ • *adj* plastikk

plate /pleɪt/ ; rett *m*; plate *f*; brett *n*; trykkplate *f* • *v* plettere; legge opp

play /pleɪ/ • *v* leke

pleas|e /pliːz, pliz/ • *adv* vær så snill • *v* behage, være til lags, tiltale **~ure** • *n* fornøyelse *m*; vellyst *f*

pluck /plʌk/ • *v* plukke, røske; ribbe; loppe

plug /plʌg/ • *n* plugg, støpsel

plus /plʌs/ • *prep* og, pluss

poem /ˈpəʊɪm, ˈpoʊəm/ • *n* dikt, episk dikt

point /pɔɪnt/ • *n* punkt *n*; komma

poised /pɔɪzd/ • *adj* tilbøyelig

poison /ˈpɔɪz(ə)n/ • *n* gift *f* **~ous** • *adj* giftig, skadelig

poke /pəʊk, poʊk/ • *v* pirke, stikke; nøre; geipe

pole /pəʊl, poʊl/ • *n* stav *m*, stokk *m*; trøe *f*; pol

polite /pəˈlaɪt/ • *adj* høflig

~ally correct • *adj* politisk korrekt, or abbr. 'P.K.'

pond /pɒnd, pɑnd/ • *n* dammen

poor /pɔː, pʊə(ɹ)/ • *adj* fattig, blakk; dårlig, elendig; stakkars

porcupine /ˈpɔː(ɹ)kjʊˌpaɪn/ • *n* hulepinnsvin

pork /pɔːk, pɔɹk/ • *n* svinekjøtt *m*

port /pɔɹt, pɔːt/ ; porting *m*; portvin *m*, port • *v* porte

portfolio /pɔɹtˈfoʊ.li.oʊ, pɔːtˈfəʊ.li.əʊ/ • *n* portefølje *m*

pose /poʊz, pəʊz/ • *v* stille, anbringe; posere; representere

position /pəˈzɪʃ(ə)n/ • *n* posisjon *m*, plassering *n* • *v* posisjonere, plassere

possess /pəˈzɛs/ • *v* inneha

possibility /ˌpɑsɪˈbɪliti, ˌpɒsɪˈbɪliti/ • *n* mulighet

post /pəʊst, poʊst/ • *v* legge ut

poster /ˈpoʊstɚ/ ; stangskudd *n*

pound /paʊnd/ • *n* pund *n*

powder /ˈpaʊ.də(ɹ)/ • *v* pulverisere, knuse; pudre

power /ˈpaʊə(ɹ), paʊ/ • *n* makt, innflytelse; kraft *m*; effekt; forsterkning **~less** • *adj* maktesløs

in ~ • *phr* i praksis

pray /pɹeɪ/ • *v* be

prayer /pɹeə(ɹ), pɹɛɚ/ ; bønnemøte *n*

preacher • *n* predikant

~cy • *n* svangerskap

prejudice /ˈpɹɛdʒədɪs/ • *n* fordom *m* **~d** • *adj* fordomsfull

prescription /pɹəˈskɹɪpʃən/ • *n* resept *m*; brilleseddel *m*

present /ˈpɹɛzənt, pɹɪˈzɛnt/ ; til stede

~cy • *n* formannskap *n*, presidentembete; presidentperiode

pretty /ˈpɹɪti, ˈpɹ̩ti/ • *adj* pen, vakker

price /pɹaɪs, pɹʌɪs/ • *n* pris *m*

prick /pɹɪk/ • *n* pikk

pride /pɹaɪd/ • *n* stolthet *m*; selvbevissthet *m*; brunst *m*; flokk *m*

print /pɹɪnt/ • *n* avtrykk *n* • *v* trykke **~er**; skriver *m*

prior /ˈpɹaɪəɹ/ • *n* prior *m*

prison /ˈpɹɪzən/ • *n* fengsel *n*

pro /pɹaʊ, pɹoʊ/ • *n* proff *m*

probe /pɹəʊb, pɹoʊb/ • *n* sonde *m* • *v* undersøke, utforske

problem /ˈpɹɒbləm, ˈpɹɑːbləm/ ; oppgave *m*; utfordring *m*

product /ˈpɹɒd.əkt, ˈpɹɑːd.əkt/ ; produkt *m*, frambringelse

proficient /pɹəˈfɪʃ.ənt, pɹoʊˈfɪʃ.ənt/ • *adj* flink

program /ˈpɹəʊɡɹæm, ˈpɹoʊˌɡɹæm/ • *n* program *n*

programme *(British)* ▷ PROGRAM

~ce • *n* prominens *m*; primærfaktor *m*

promis|e /ˈpɹɒmɪs, ˈpɹɑːmɪs/ • *n* løfte *n* • *v* love

prompt /pɹɒmpt, pɹɑːmpt/ • *adj* prompt, prompte **~ly** • *adv* prompt, prompte

pron|ounce /pɹəˈnaʊns/ • *v* erklære; uttale **~unciation** • *n* uttale *m*

proper /ˈpɹɒp.ə, ˈpɹɑː.pə/ • *adj* passende, høvelig; ordentlig, veloppdragent, høvisk; egentlig; riktig, korrekt; egen; skikkelig; sann

property /ˈpɹɒp.ət.i, ˈpɹɑːp.ət.i/ ; tomt *f*

propos|e /pɹəˈpəʊz, pɹəˈpoʊz/ • *v* foreslå; fri

protect /pɹəˈtɛkt/ • *v* beskytte, verne, sikre, dekke, gardere

protest /ˈpɹəʊ.tɛst, ˈpɹoʊ.tɛst/ • *v* protestere

proud /pɹaʊd/ • *adj* stolt

province /ˈpɹɒvɪns, ˈpɹɑːvɪns/ • *n* provins *m*

provo|ke /pɹəˈvəʊk, pɹəˈvoʊk/ • *v* provosere

psychology /saɪˈkɒlədʒi, saɪˈkɑːlədʒɪ/ ; psykologi

public /ˈpʌblɪk/ • *adj* offentlig, allmenn, allmennt

publish /ˈpʌblɪʃ/ • *v* publisere

pull /pʊl/ • *v* trekke, dra; trekke tilbake; gjennomføre

punish /ˈpʌnɪʃ/ • *v* straffe

punk /pʌŋk, pəŋk/ • *n* pønk *m*, punk *m*; pønker *m*, punker *m*

puny /pjuːni/ • *adj* ynkelig

pupil /pjuːpəl/ ; pupill *m*

purchase /ˈpɜːtʃəs, ˈpɜːtʃəs/ • *n* kjøp *n*, anskaffelse *m*; overdragelse *m*, ervervelse *m* • *v* kjøpe, anskaffe, erverve; sikre seg, kjøpe seg **~** • *n* kjøp *n*, anskaffelse *m*; overdragelse *m*, ervervelse *m*

● *v* kjøpe, anskaffe, erverve; sikre seg, kjøpe seg

pure /ˈpjʊə, ˈpjʊɪ/ ● *adj* pur, ren

purple /ˈpɜ:(ɪ).pəl, ˈpɜ́pəl/ ● *n* lilla, fiolett

purpose /ˈpɜ́pəs, ˈpɜ:pəs/ ● *n* mål *n* **on** ~ ● *phr* med vilje, med overlegg

purr /pɜ:(ɪ)/ ● *v* male

purse /pɜ:s, pɜ́s/ ● *n* pung, pengepung

push /pʊʃ/ ● *v* dytte, skubbe

put /pʊt/ ● *v* sette; ordlegge ~ **sth out** ● *adj* satt ut ● *v* sette ut, slippe ut; lage, produsere; slokke, slukke

~ing ● *adj* forunderlig

Qatar ● *n* Qatar

quality /ˈkwɒlɪti, ˈkwælɪti/ ● *n* kvalitet

quarrel /ˈkwɒɪəl, ˈkwɒɪəl/ ● *n* krangel *m* ● *v* krangle

quarter /ˈkwɔ:tə, ˈk(w)ɔɪ.tə/ ; bydel, kvarter

queen /kwi:n/ ● *n* dronning *f*; dame, dama *f*

quick /kwɪk/ ● *adj* rask, kvikk; frisk og rask **~ly** ● *adv* fort

quiet /ˈkwaɪ.ɪt, ˈkwaɪ.ət/ ; rolig

quit /kwɪt/ ● *adj* slutte

quite /kwaɪt/ ● *adv* temmelig; helt; ganske

quitted *(sp/pp)* ▷ QUIT

quot|e /kwəʊt/ ● *v* sitere

rabbit /ˈɹæbɪt, ˈɹæbəɹ/ ● *n* kanin *m*

radiation /ˌɹeɪ.di.ˈeɪ.ʃən, ˌɹaɪ.di.ˈaɪ.ʃən/ ● *n* utstråling; stråling

rage /ɹeɪdʒ/ ● *v* rase

rail /ɹeɪl/ ● *n* rekkverk, gelender; skinne; sprosse, slå

rain /ɹeɪn/ ● *n* regn *n*, regnvær *n* ● *v* regne

rally /ˈɹæ.li/ ● *n* ballveksling *m* ● *v* regruppere; samle seg, fylke seg; komme seg, komme til krefter

ran *(sp)* ▷ RUN

random /ˈɹændəm/ ● *adj* tilfeldig, tilfellelig, tilfelleleg

rang *(sp)* ▷ RING

rapid /ˈɹæpɪd/ ● *adj* rask, hurtig

rare /ɹɛə, ɹɛəɹ/ ● *adj* skjelden

rate /ɹeɪt/ ● *n* hyppighet, prosent, tall

rather /ˈɹɑːðə, ˌɹɑːˈðː(ɪ)/ ● *adv* heller, fortrinnsvis; ganske, nokså, temmelig

ratio /ˈɹeɪʃ(i)ˌoʊ/ ● *n* forhold *n*

raven /ˈɹeɪvən/ ● *adj* ravnsort, ravnsvart ● *n* ravn *m*

ray /ɹeɪ/ ; rokke

reach /ɹi:tʃ/ ● *v* rekke

read /ɹid, ɹiːd/ ● *v* (*sp* read, *pp* read) lese; forstå, høre, oppfatte; studere

ready /ˈɹɛdi/ • *adj* klar, parat;
beredt, rede

real /ˈɹiːəl/ • *adj* virkelig **~ly** •
adv veldig

realm /ɹɛlm/ • *n* rike

reason /ˈɹiːzən/ ; fornuft • *v*
resonnere, overveie; diskutere
fornuftig **~able**; fornuftig

receipt /ɹɪˈsiːt/ ; kvittering;
oppskrift

receive /ɹɪˈsiːv/ • *v* få; ta imot **~r**
• *n* mottaker *m*; heler *m*

recent /ˈɹiːsənt/ • *adj* nylig

recipe /ˈɹɛs.ɪ.pi/ • *n* oppskrift *f*

reconcil|e /ˈɹɛkənsaɪl/ • *v*
forsone **~iation** • *n*
avstemming *m*

record /ˈɹɛkɔːd, ˈɹɛkəd/ • *v* spille
inn

red /ɹɛd/ • *adj* rød; rødlig • *n* rød

reduc|e /ɹɪˈdjuːs, ɹɪˈduːs/ • *v*
redusere **~tion** • *n* reduksjon
m

refrigerator /ɹɪˈfɹɪdʒəˌɹeɪtə,
ɹɪˈfɹɪdʒəˌɹeɪtɚ/ • *n* kjøleskap *n*

regard /ɹɪˈɡɑːd, ɹɪˈɡɑɹd/ • *n*
respekt *m*, aktelse *m*;
betraktning

region /ˈɹiːdʒn/ • *n* region

regret /ɹɪˈɡɹɛt/ • *n* beklagelse

regular /ˈɹɛɡjʊlə, ˈɹɛɡjəlɚ/ • *adj*
regelmessig

regulation • *n* regulering

rehearsal • *n* øvelse *f*, øving *f*

reign /ɹeɪn/ • *n* maktutøvelse *m*
• *v* regjere

reject /ɹɪˈdʒɛkt, ˈɹiːdʒɛkt/ • *v*
avslå, avvise

~onship; forhold

relax /ɹɪˈlæks/ • *v* slappe av

relevant /ˈɹɛləvənt/ • *adj* relevant

~us • *adj* religiøs

rel|y /ɹɪˈlaɪ/ • *v* lite på

remote /ɹɪˈməʊt, ɹɪˈmoʊt/ • *adj*
fjern • *n* fjernkontroll *m*

renowned • *adj* berømt,
vidgjeten

repair /ɹɪˈpɛə, ɹɪˈpɛɚ/ • *n*
reparasjon *m*, reparering *f* • *v*
reparere

reply /ɹɪˈplaɪ/ • *n* svar *n* • *v* svare

represent /ɹɛp.ɹɪˈzɛnt/ • *v*
representere

requirement /ɹɪˈkwʌɪəm(ə)nt,
ɹɪˈkwaɪɹmənt/ • *n* krav

resembl|e /ɹɪˈzɛmb(ə)l/ • *v* likne,
minne om

reserv|e /ɹɪˈzɜːv, ɹɪˈzɝːv/ • *n*
bestilling, reservering,
reservasjon *m*; reserverthet *m*,
tilbakeholdenhet *m*; reservat
n; reservetropp *m*; forråd *n*,
reservefond • *v* holde av,
reservere, sette av;
forbeholde, legge til side;
bestille **~ed**; reservert **~ation**
• *n* forbehold

residen|ce /ˈɹɛz.ɪ.dəns/ ; bolig *m*
~t • *n* beboer

resign /ɹɪˈzaɪn/ • *v* gå av, si opp;
gi opp, resignere

resist /ɹɪˈzɪst/ • *v* motstå **~ance**
• *n* motstand *m*; motkraft *f*;
resistans *m*

~ion • *n* vedtak *n*

resort /ɹɪˈzɔː(ɹ)t/ • *v* ty til

~ility • *n* ansvar *n*

restaurant /ˈɹɛs.t(ə).ɹɒ̃,
ˈɹɛs.t(ə)ˌɹɑnt/ • *n* restaurant *m*

result /ɹɪˈzʌlt/ ; resultat *n*, utfall *n*

retain /ɹɪˈteɪn/ • *v* få, motta

R

reve|al /ɹəˈviːl/ • v avsløre
~lation; åpenbaring m
revenge /ɹɪˈvɛndʒ/ • n hevn
review /ɹɪˈvjuː/ • n anmeldelse m
reward /ɹɪˈwɔːd/ • n belønning
Reykjavik • n Reykjavík,
Reykjavik
ridded (sp/pp) ▷ RID
ridden (pp) ▷ RIDE
ride /ɹaɪd/ ; ri
ridge /ɹɪdʒ/ • n møne n; rygg m,
åsrygg m
~ now • adv akkurat nå
ring /ɹɪŋ/ • n ring m • v (sp rang,
pp rung) ringe; telefonere
rise /ɹaɪz, ɹaɪs/ • n risa
risen (pp) ▷ RISE
river /ˈɹɪvə, ˈɹɪvər/ • n flod m, elv f,
å m
road /ɹəʊd, ɹoʊd/ • n vei m, veg m
rock /ɹɒk, ɹɑk/ ; klippe m;
kampestein m; bergart m;
edelstein m; isbit m;
kandissukker m; crack • v
gynge; riste; ryste, sjokkere
rocket /ˈɹɒkɪt, ˈɹɒkɪt/ • n rakett m
rode (sp) ▷ RIDE
role /ɹəʊl/ • n rolle m
roll /ɹəʊl, ɹoʊl/ • v knipse
Romania • n Romania
roof /ɹuːf/ • n tak n
room /ɹuːm, ɹʊm/ • n rom n,
plass m; værelse n ~mate • n
romkamerat m
rooster /ˈɹuːstə, ˈɹʊstər/ • n hane
m
root /ɹuːt, ɹʊt/ • v rote
• (also) ▷ RISE
round /ˈɹaʊnd/ • adj rund ~ up •
v samle
route /ɹuːt, ɹuːt/ • n rute f

rubber /ˈɹʌbə(ɹ), ˈɹʌbər/ ;
kunstgummi m; gummi m,
kondom m; kalosj m; dekk n,
bilgummi m
ruby • n rubin m
rude /ɹuːd, ɹud/ • adj
uforskammet; grov; rå
rumor /ˈɹuːmə(ɹ), ˈɹuːmər/ • n rykte
rumour (British) ▷ RUMOR
run /ɹʌn, ɹʊn/ • n Løpe • v (sp
ran, pp run) løpe, springe; gå
~ away • v stikke av ~ into
sb/sth • v kjøre på en ~ over
sb/sth • v kjøre over, kjøre
ned
rung (pp) ▷ RING
Russia • n Russland
rust /ɹʌst/ • v ruste
ruthless /ˈɹuːθləs/ • adj
hensynsløs, ubarmhjertig
Rwanda • n Rwanda

S

sack /sæk/ ; sparken • v plyndre
sacred /ˈseɪkɹɪd/ • adj hellig
sacrifice /ˈsækɹɪfaɪs/ ; offer n • v
ofre
sad /sæd/ • adj trist, lei seg
~ness • n melankoli m
safe /seɪf/ • adj sikker, trygg • n
safe m ~ly • adv trygt ~guard
• n sikring f
said (sp/pp) ▷ SAY
sail /seɪl/ • n seil; seiltur • v
seile ~ing • adj seilende ~or
• n matros m, sjømann m

saint /seɪnt, sən(t)/ • *v*
kanonisere

sake /seɪk/ • *n* sake *m* **for God's
~** • *interj* for Guds skyld,
Gudskjelov

salad /'sæləd/ • *n* salat *m*

sale /seɪl/ ; auksjon *m* **on ~** • *phr*
til salgs

salmon /'sæmən, 'sælmən/ • *n* (*pl*
salmon) laksfisk *m*, laks *m*

salt /sɔːlt, sɒlt/ • *n* salt *n*,
bordsalt *n* • *v* salte

sample /'sɑːm.pəl, 'sæm.pəl/ • *n*
prøve, sample, eksempel • *v*
ta prøve av

sanction /'sæŋkʃən/ • *n*
godkjennelse *m*, tillatelse *m*;
sanksjon *m* • *v* godkjenne,
tillate; sanksjonere, straffe

sand /sænd/ ; sandstrand,
strand; sandfarget **~y**;
sandfarget

sang (*sp*) ▷ SING

sank (*sp*) ▷ SINK

sat (*sp/pp*) ▷ SIT

satellite /'sætəlaɪt/ • *n* satelitt

satisf|y /'sætɪsfaɪ/ • *v*
tilfredsstille **~ied** • *adj*
tilfreds, fornøyd, mett

Saturn • *n* Saturn *m*
~y • *adj* frekk; dristig

sav|e /seɪv/ • *n* redning • *prep*
unntatt • *v* redde; spare, lagre
~ing • *n* økonomisering

saw /sɔː, sɒ/ • *v* (*sp* sawed, *pp*
sawn) sage • (*also*) ▷ SEE

sawed (*sp/pp*) ▷ SAW

sawn (*pp*) ▷ SAW

scam /skæm/ • *n* bondefangeri

scar /skɑː, skɑː(ɹ)/ • *n* arr *n*

scared /skɛəd, skɛːɹd/ • *adj* redd,
skremt

scarf /skɑːf, skɑːɹf/ • *n* (*pl*
scarves) skjerf *n*

scarlet /'skɑːlɪt, 'skɑːlɪt/ • *n*
skarlagen *n*

scarves (*pl*) ▷ SCARF

scatter /'skætə, 'skætɚ/ ; strø

scene /siːn/ • *n* scene **~ry** • *n*
landskap, scene

sceptical (*British*) ▷ SKEPTICAL

schedule /'ʃed.juːl, 'ske.dʒʊl/ • *n*
timeplan *m*

school /skul, skuːl/ • *n* fakultet *n*;
skole *m* • *v* skole, skolere,
lære opp, utdanne

scien|ce /'saɪəns/ ; kunskap

score /skɔː, skɔɹ/ • *n* poengsum
m; partitur *n*

scorpion /'skɔː.pi.ən, 'skɔɹ.pi.ən/ •
n skorpion *m*

scratch /skɹætʃ/ • *n* risp *n*

scrawny • *adj* tynn, radmager,
skrinn/skrant, skranglet

scream /skɹiːm, skɹiːm/ • *v*
skrike, hyle

screw /skɹuː/ • *n* skrue *m*;
skruing *m* **~driver** • *n*
skrujern, skrutrekker;
screwdriver *m*

scrutin|y /'skɹuː.tɪ.ni/ • *n*
finlesing **~ize** • *v* granske

seal /siːl/ • *n* sel *m*; forsegling *m*;
segl *n*

search /sɜːtʃ, sɜːtʃ/ ; lete

season /'siː.zən, 'sizən/ • *n* årstid
f, sesong *m*; løpetid *f* • *v*
krydre, smaksette; modnes

seat /siːt/ • *n* sete

second /'sekənd, 'sek.(ə)nd/ • *adj*
andre *n*; sekund *n*; øyeblikk *n*;

S

sekundant *m*; støtte; feilvare *m*

secre|t /ˈsiːkɪt, ˈsiːkɹət/ • *adj* hemmelig, skjult

section /ˈsɛkʃən/ • *v* tvangsinnlegge

secur|e /səˈkjʊə(ɹ), səˈkjʊɹ/ • *adj* sikker

see /siː/ ; skjønne, forstå

~er • *n* søker

seen *(pp)* ▷ SEE

seiz|e /siːz/ • *v* gripe **~ure** • *n* inndragning *m*; krampe *f*

self /sɛlf/ • *n* (*pl* selves) selv

sell /sɛl/ • *v* (*sp* sold, *pp* sold) selge; få solgt, bli solgt

selves *(pl)* ▷ SELF

senate /ˈsɛnɪt/ • *n* senat

send /sɛnd/ • *v* (*sp* sent, *pp* sent) sende

Senegal • *n* Senegal

sense /sɛn(t)s, sɪn(t)s/ • *n* sans *m*

sensitive /ˈsɛnsɪtɪv/ • *adj* følsom

sent *(sp/pp)* ▷ SEND

sentence /ˈsɛntəns/ ; dom *m*; straff *m*; setning • *v* dømme

separate /ˈsɛp(ə)ɹət, ˈsɛpəɹeɪt/ • *v* skille, avsondre

~n; serbisk

series /ˈsɪə.ɹiːz, ˈsɪɹiz/ • *n* (*pl* series) serie *f*; rekke *f*

serious /ˈsɪəɹi.əs/ • *adj* alvorlig, seriøs **~ly** • *adv* serr, seriøst

serv|e /sɜːv, sɜv/ • *v* tjene; servere

set /sɛt/ • *v* (*sp* set, *pp* set) gå ned; bestemme, fastlegge; stille, justere; dekke; introdusert; sette, plassere; sette sammen; stille opp; stivne, størkne; putte

seven /ˈsɛv.ən/ • *n* sjutall *n*, syvtall *n* • *num* sju, syv **~teen** • *num* sytten **~ty** • *num* sytti

sewed *(sp/pp)* ▷ SEW

sewn *(pp)* ▷ SEW

sex /sɛks/ ; kjønn *n* **~y** • *adj* sexy, kjønnslig, seksuell

shadow /ˈʃædoʊ, ˈʃædəʊ/ • *n* skygge *m*

shake /ʃeɪk/ • *v* (*sp* shook, *pp* shaken) riste; handhilse; shake

shaken *(pp)* ▷ SHAKE

shall /ˈʃæl, ʃəl/ • *v* (*sp* should, *pp* -) skal; skulle

shame /ʃeɪm/ • *n* skam

share /ʃɛə, ʃɛəɹ/ • *n* aksje *m* • *v* dele **~holder** • *n* aksjonær, aksjeeier

sharp /ʃɑːp, ʃɑɹp/ • *adj* skarp; smart; spiss; -iss

shat *(sp)* ▷ SHIT

she /ʃiː, ʃi/ • *pron* hun *f*

shear /ʃɪə(ɹ), ʃɪɹ/ • *n* bøylesaks; klipp *m* • *v* (*sp* sheared, *pp* shorn) klippe

sheared *(sp/pp)* ▷ SHEAR

shed /ʃɛd/ • *n* skur *m*

sheep /ʃip, ʃiːp/ • *n* (*pl* sheep) sau *m*, får *n*

sheet /ʃiːt, ʃit/ • *n* papir

shell /ʃɛl/ • *n* skjell

shelter /ˈʃɛltə, ˈʃɛltəɹ/ • *n* ly

shelves *(pl)* ▷ SHELF

shine /ʃaɪn/ • *v* (*sp* shone, *pp* shone) lyse

shit /ʃɪt/ • *interj* faen! • *n* dritt *m*, skitt *m*, avføring *m*, bæsj *m*, skit *m*, møkk, ekskrement *n*, lort *m* • *v* (*sp* shit, *pp* shit) skite, bæsje

shitted *(sp/pp)* ▷ SHIT

shiver /ˈʃɪvəɹ, ˈʃɪvə/ • *v* skjelve

shod *(sp/pp)* ▷ SHOE

~lace • *n* skolisse *f*

shoed *(sp/pp)* ▷ SHOE

shone *(sp)* ▷ SHINE

shook *(sp)* ▷ SHAKE

shoot /ʃuːt/ • *v* *(sp* shot, *pp* shot) skyte

shop /ʃɒp, ʃɑp/ • *n* butikk *m*, forretning *m*; sløyd *m* • *v* handle, shoppe **~ping** • *n* shopping *m*, handling *m*; varer, matvarer

shorn *(pp)* ▷ SHEAR

shot /ʃɒt, ʃɑt/ • *n* hagl *n* • *(also)* ▷ SHOOT

should /ʃʊd, ʃəd/ • *v* burde; skulle • *(also)* ▷ SHALL

shout /ʃaʊt, ʃʌʊt/ • *n* rop *m* • *v* rope

show /ʃəʊ, ʃoʊ/ • *n* show *m*, program *m* • *v* vise *(sp* showed, *pp* shown)

showed *(sp/pp)* ▷ SHOW

shown *(pp)* ▷ SHOW

shrank *(sp)* ▷ SHRINK

shredded *(sp/pp)* ▷ SHRED

shrink /ʃɹɪŋk/ • *v* *(sp* shrank, *pp* shrunk) krympe

shrunk *(sp/pp)* ▷ SHRINK

shuttle /ˈʃʌɾel/ • *n* skyttel *m*; skytteltrafikk

shy /ʃaɪ/ • *adj* sjenert

sibling /ˈsɪblɪŋ/ • *n* søsken *n*

sick /sɪk/ • *n* syke

side /saɪd/ • *n* side *m*, kant *m*; lag *n*

Sierra Leone • *n* Sierra Leone

sigh /saɪ/ • *n* sukk *n* • *v* sukke

signature /ˈsɪgnətʃə, ˈsɪgnətʃəɹ/ • *n* underskrift *f*, signatur *m*

silen|t /ˈsaɪlənt/ ; stum **~tly** • *adv* stille **~ce** • *interj* stille!, hysj! • *n* ro *m*, taushet *m*, togn • *v* roe

silly /ˈsɪli/ • *adj* tullete, fjollete

silver /ˈsɪl.və, ˈsɪl.vəɹ/ ; sølv

simpl|y /ˈsɪmpli/ • *adv* rett og slett, ganske enkelt, intet mindre enn **~ify**; forenkles

simultaneous /ˌsɪm.əlˈteɪm.i.əs, ˌsaɪm.əlˈteɪm.i.əs/ • *adj* samtidig, samstundes **~ly** • *adv* samtidig

~ful • *adj* syndig

since /sɪn(t)s/ • *conj* siden; fordi, da • *prep* siden

sincere /sɪnˈsɪə(ɹ)/ • *adj* oppriktig

sing /sɪŋ/ • *v* *(sp* sang, *pp* sung) synge

Singapore • *n* Singapore

sink /sɪŋk/ • *v* *(sp* sank, *pp* sunk) synke; senke

sister /ˈsɪs.tə, ˈsɪs.təɹ/ • *n* søster, storesøster, lillesøster

sit /sɪt/ • *v* *(sp* sat, *pp* sat) sitte; sette seg

six /sɪks/ • *num* seks **~teen** • *num* seksten **~th** • *adj* sjette **~ty** • *num* seksti

ski /skiː, ʃiː/ • *v* gå på ski

~ful • *adj* skikket

skin /skɪn/ • *n* hud *m*, skinn *n*, ham *m*

skirt /skɜːt, skɜt/ • *n* skjørt *n*

skull /skʌl/ • *n* skalle *m*, skolt *m*, haus *m*

skunk /skʌŋk/ • *n* skunk *m*, stinkdyr *n*

sky /skaɪ/ • *n* himmel *m*
~scraper • *n* skyskraper
slam /slæm/ • *v* slå til
slap • *n* ørefik *m*, en over kjeften
• *v* fike, slå
slash /slaʃ, slæʃ/ • *n* skråstrek *m*
slave /sleɪv/ ; sexslave *m*,
seksualslave *m*
sleep /sliːp, slip/ • *n* søvn *m* • *v*
(*sp* slept, *pp* slept) sove ~ **over**
• *v* natte over *m*, overnatte **~y**
• *adj* trøtt, døsig, søvnig
slept (*sp/pp*) ▷ SLEEP
slice /slaɪs/ • *v* å skjære
slid (*sp/pp*) ▷ SLIDE
slide /slaɪd/ • *n* ras *n*; sleide *m* •
v (*sp* slid, *pp* slid) gli, skli
sling /slɪŋ/ • *v* (*sp* slung, *pp*
slung) slynge
slip /slɪp/ • *v* skli, gli
slope /sloʊp, sləʊp/ • *n* skråning
f, bakke *m*, oppoverbakke *m*,
nedoverbakke *m*; stigning *m*,
helling *f*
sloth /sləʊθ, slɔθ/ • *n* latskap *m*,
lediggang *m*
Slovenia • *n* Slovenia
slow /sləʊ, sloʊ/ • *adj* langsom *f*,
langsomt *n*, langsomme **~ly** •
adv sakte, langsomt
slung (*sp/pp*) ▷ SLING
small /smɔːl, smɔl/ • *adj* liten;
ung
smell /smɛl/ • *v* (*sp* smelt, *pp*
smelt) lukte; stinke
smelled (*sp/pp*) ▷ SMELL
smelt (*sp/pp*) ▷ SMELL
smile /smaɪl/ • *n* smil *n*
smok|e /sməʊk, smoʊk/ • *n* røyk
m

snake /sneɪk/ • *n* slange *m*, orm
m; stakefjær
sneak /sniːk/ • *n* snik *m* • *v* snike
snow /snəʊ, snoʊ/ ; snø; snøfall *n*
so /səʊ, soʊ/ • *adv* så; slik • *conj*
så
soccer /'sɒk.ə, 'sɑk.ɚ/ • *n* fotball
m
socia|l /'səʊʃəl, 'soʊ.ʃəl/ • *adj*
sosial • *n* sosialen
society /sə'saɪ.ə.ti/ • *n* samfunn *n*
sock /sɒk, sɑk/ • *n* sokk *m*
sofa /'soʊfə, 'səʊfə/ • *n* sofa
soft /sɒft, sɑft/ • *adj* svak, myk;
forsiktig; bløt **~en** • *v*
bløtgjøre
software /'sɒft,wɛə, 'sɑft,wɛɹ/ • *n*
programvare *f*
soil /sɔɪl/ ; jordsmonn *n*
sold (*sp/pp*) ▷ SELL
sole /səʊl, soʊl/ • *adj* eneste;
singel, enslig; sjøtunge *f* • *v*
såle **~ly** • *adv* bare
solid /'sɑlɪd, 'sɒlɪd/ • *adj* fast;
solid, kraftig; massiv,
kompakt; sammenskriving
some /sʌm, sɛm/ • *adv* omtrent
• *pron* visse **~thing**; noenting
~times • *adv* stundom, av og
til, tidvis **~what** • *adv* noen
lunde
son /sʌn/ • *n* sønn *m*
soon /suːn/ • *adv* snart
sorry /'sɔɹi, 'sɒɹi/ • *adj* lei;
sørgelig; unnskyld
sort /sɔːt, sɔɹt/ • *v* sortere
sought (*sp/pp*) ▷ SEEK
soul /səʊl, soʊl/ • *n* sjel *f*
sound /saʊnd/ • *adj* sunn, frisk;
stødig; grei • *n* lyd *m*
sour /'saʊ(ə)ɹ, 'saʊə/ • *adj* sur

S

South Africa ● *n* Sør-Afrika, Republikken Sør-Afrika

South Sudan ● *n* Sør-Sudan

sow /saʊ/ ● *v* (*sp* sowed, *pp* sown) så

sowed *(sp/pp)* ▷ SOW

sown *(pp)* ▷ SOW

space /speɪs/ ● *n* rom

Spa|in ● *n* Spania

spam /'spæm/ ● *n* søppelpost *m* ● *v* sende søppelpost

spark /spɑːk, spɑːk/ ; gnist *m*

sparkling ● *adj* glitre

spat *(sp/pp)* ▷ SPIT

speak /spiːk, spik/ ● *v* (*sp* spoke, *pp* spoken) snakke

special /'speʃəl/ ; spesiell **~ty** ● *n* spesialitet **~ist** ● *n* spesialist **~cles** ● *n* briller

sped *(sp/pp)* ▷ SPEED

speech /spiːtʃ/ ● *n* tale *m*, stemme *m*

speed /spiːd/ ● *n* hastighet *f* ● *v* (*sp* sped, *pp* sped) råkjøre; kjøre over fartsgrensen; flå

speeded *(sp/pp)* ▷ SPEED

spell /spel/ ● *n* trylleformel *m*, formel *m*, besvergelse *m* ● *v* (*sp* spelt, *pp* spelt) stave

spelled *(sp/pp)* ▷ SPELL

spelt *(sp/pp)* ▷ SPELL

spend /spend/ ● *n* lommepenger ● *v* (*sp* spent, *pp* spent) bruke

spent *(sp/pp)* ▷ SPEND

spin /spɪn/ ● *n* spinn *n* ● *v* (*sp* spun, *pp* spun) spinne

spine /spaɪn/ ; rygg *m*; ryggrad *m*

spirit /'spɪrɪt, 'spɪrɪt/ ● *n* ånd *m*, sjel *f* **~ual** ● *adj* åndelig, spirituell

spoil /spɔɪl/ ● *v* (*sp* spoilt, *pp* spoilt) forderve

spoiled *(sp/pp)* ▷ SPOIL

spoilt *(sp/pp)* ▷ SPOIL

spoke *(sp)* ▷ SPEAK

spot /spɒt, spɑt/ ● *n* flekk, prikk; kvise; sted *n* ● *v* oppdage, identifisere; låne

sprang *(sp)* ▷ SPRING

spread /sprɛd/ ● *v* (*sp* spread, *pp* spread) spre

spring /sprɪŋ/ ● *n* vår *m*

sprung *(pp)* ▷ SPRING

spun *(sp/pp)* ▷ SPIN

spy /spaɪ/ ● *v* spionere; få øye på

squeamish /'skwiːmɪʃ/ ● *adj* pysete

squeeze /skwiːz/ ● *v* trykke, klemme, presse, kveste, knuse

squid /skwɪd/ ● *n* (*pl* squid) akkar *m*

stab /stæb/ ● *n* stikk *n* ● *v* stikke

stab|le /'steɪ.bəl/ ● *adj* stabil ● *n* stall *m*; fjøs *n*

stack /stæk/ ● *n* stakk

staff /stɑːf, 'stæf/ ● *n* stav; personale

stage /steɪdʒ/ ● *n* scene, skueplass

stain /steɪn/ ● *v* sverte

stair /steər, steə/ ● *n* trinn *n*; trapp *f*

stake /steɪk/ ● *n* stake *m*, påle *m*; aksje *m*; interesse *m*, risiko *m*

stance /stɑːns, stæns/ ● *n* kroppsholdning *m*; standpunkt *n*

stand /stænd, æ/ ● *v* (*sp* stood, *pp* stood) stå, bli stående;

motstå; reise opp; tåle; reise seg, stå opp

stank /sp/ ▷ STINK

star /stɑː(ɹ), stɑɹ/ ; kjendis *m* **~fish** • *n* sjøstjerne

start /stɑːt, stɑɹt/ • *v* starte; begynne

state /steɪt/ ; tilstand

station /ˈsteɪʃən/ • *v* stasjonere

statistics /stəˈtɪstɪks/ • *n* statistikk

status /ˈsteɪt.əs, ˈstæt.əs/ • *n* status *m*

stay /steɪ/ • *v* bli, forbli

steadfast /ˈstɛdfæst/ • *adj* stødig; traust

steak /steɪk/ • *n* steik, stek *m*

steal /stiːl/ • *n* kupp *n*; stjele; liste seg

steep /stiːp/ • *adj* bratt

step /stɛp/ ; trin; skritt *n*, steg *n*

stern /stɜn, stɜːn/ • *n* akterende *m*

stick /stɪk/ • *n* kvist *m*; kjepp *m*; stokk *m*; hockeykølle *m*; girspak *m*

still /stɪl/ • *adj* stille; likevel, enda • *n* destillasjonsapparat *n* • *v* roe, stille

sting /stɪŋ/ • *n* stikk *n* • *v* (*sp* stung, *pp* stung) stikke **~er** • *n* brodd *m*

stingy /ˈstɪndʒi/ • *adj* gjerrig

stole *(sp)* ▷ STEAL

stolen *(pp)* ▷ STEAL

stomach /ˈstʌmək/ ; mage *m*, buk *m*

stone /stəʊn, stoʊn/ • *adj* steinaktig • *n* stein *m*; edelstein *m* • *v* steine

stood *(sp/pp)* ▷ STAND

store /stɔɹ, stɔː/ • *n* lager *n*; forråd *m* • *v* oppbevare; lagre; holde **~age** • *n* lager *n*

story /ˈstɔː.ɹi/ • *n* historie *m*

straight /stɹeɪt/ • *adj* heterofil

strain /stɹeɪn/ • *v* sile

strand /stɹænd/ • *n* strand *m*

strange /stɹeɪndʒ/ • *adj* merkelig, sær, rar, selsom; ukjent

stress /stɹɛs/ • *n* stress *n*

strike /stɹaɪk/ • *n* streik *m* • *v* (*sp* struck, *pp* struck) stryke; slå, ramme; streike

string /stɹɪŋ/ • *n* streng *m*

strive /stɹaɪv/ • *v* (*sp* strove, *pp* striven) streve

striven *(pp)* ▷ STRIVE

stroke /stɹəʊk, stɹoʊk/ • *n* slag *n*; tak *n*; strøk *n*

strove *(sp)* ▷ STRIVE

struck *(sp/pp)* ▷ STRIKE

struggle /ˈstɹʌgl/ • *v* slåss, kjempe, slite streve

strung *(sp/pp)* ▷ STRING

stuck *(sp/pp)* ▷ STICK

study /ˈstʌdi/ ; arbeidsrom • *v* studere, lære

stuff /stʌf/ • *n* ting, saker; stoff *n*, materiale *n* • *v* stappe, fylle

stun /stʌn/ • *v* svimeslå, lamslå, lamme

stung *(sp/pp)* ▷ STING

stunk *(sp/pp)* ▷ STINK

stupid /ˈstjuːpɪd, ˈst(j)upɪd/ • *adj* dum

style /staɪl/ • *n* stil; tiltaleform *m* • *v* stilisere; tiltale

subsidiary /sʌbˈsɪ.di.əɹ.i/ • *adj* subsidiær

substan|ce /ˈsʌbstəns/ • *n*
substans *m*, masse *m*; formue
m; narkotika **~tially** • *adv* i alt
vesentligt, vesentligen

succinct /sə(k)ˈsɪŋkt, sək'sɪŋ(k)t/
• *adj* konsis

suck /sʌk, sʊk/ • *v* suge

suffer /ˈsʌfə, ˈsʌfər/ • *v* lide;
forverre

suffice /səˈfaɪs/ • *v* rekke

suffix /ˈsʌfɪks/ • *v* suffigere

sugar /ˈʃʊgə(ɹ), ˈʃʊgər/ • *n* sukker
n; kjære *m*

~ion • *n* forslag *n*

suicide /ˈs(j)uːɪˌsaɪd, ˈs(j)uːɪˌsaɪd/ •
n selvmord *n*; selvmordsoffer
n

suitable /ˈsuːtəbl/ • *adj*
passende, egnet

sulky • *adj* sur • *n* sulky *m*

sullen /ˈsʌlən/ • *adj* muggen, utilfreds,
trist

sum /sʌm/ ; sum

summary /ˈsʌmərɪ/ • *n* resumé *n*

summer /ˈsʌmə(ɹ), ˈsʌmər/ • *n*
sommer

summon /ˈsʌmən/ • *v* tilkalle

sun /sʌn/ • *n* sol

sung *(pp)* ▷ SING

sunk *(pp)* ▷ SINK

super /ˈs(j)uːpə(ɹ), ˈs(j)uːpər/ • *adj*
super

supercilious /ˌsjuːːpə(ɹ)ˈsɪ.li.əs,
ˌs(j)uːpəˈsɪli.əs/ • *adj* hovmodig

support /səˈpɔːt, səˈpɔɹt/ • *n*
støtte; bistand

suppose /səˈpəʊz, səˈpoʊz/ • *v*
anta, formode; forutsette

~ly • *adv* sikkert; trygt

surge|ry /ˈsɜːdʒəɹi, ˈsɜːdʒəɹi/ • *n*
operasjon *m*; kirurgi *m* **~on** •
n kirurg *m*

Suriname • *n* Surinam

surpris|e /səˈpɹaɪz, səˈpɹaɪz/ ;
overrasknings-,
overraskelses-; overraskelse
m • *v* overraske

surviv|e /səˈvaɪv, səˈvaɪv/ • *v*
overleve; leve lenger enn **~or**
• *n* overlever *m*

suspicio|us /səˈspɪ.ʃəs/ • *adj*
suspekt **~n** • *n* mistanke *m*

suspen|d /səˈspɛnd/ • *v*
suspendere; henge; avbryte

~able • *adj* bærekraftig

swam *(sp)* ▷ SWIM

sweat /swɛt/ • *v* *(sp* sweat, *pp*
sweat) svette

sweated *(sp/pp)* ▷ SWEAT

sweet /swiːt, swiːt/ • *adj* ren; søt;
sukkertilsatt; usaltet, fersk;
søtlig; vakker; snill, vennlig;
hjelpsom

swelled *(sp/pp)* ▷ SWELL

swept *(sp/pp)* ▷ SWEEP

switch /swɪtʃ/ ; prylestokk *m*;
svitsj *m*; sentral *m*

Swi|tzerland • *n* Sveits

swollen *(pp)* ▷ SWELL

swore *(sp)* ▷ SWEAR

sworn *(pp)* ▷ SWEAR

swum *(pp)* ▷ SWIM

swung *(sp/pp)* ▷ SWING

S

T

table 50 thin

table /'teɪbəl/ • *n* bord *n*; tabell *m*
• *v* dekke bordet **~spoon** • *n*
suppeskje

tablet computer • *n* nettbrett *n*

tag /tæg, teɪg/ • *n* etikett *m*,
merkelapp *m*; sisten; tagg *m*;
tag *m*

tail /teɪl/ ; hale *m*; forfølger *m* • *v*
forfølge, skygge

Tajikistan • *n* Tadsjikistan

take /teɪk/ • *n* fangst *m*; gevinst
m; opptak *n*; mottak *n* • *v* (*sp*
took, *pp* taken) bringe; ta;
gripe; tåle; voldta **~ off** • *v* ta
av

taken *(pp)* ▷ TAKE

tale /teɪl/ • *n* historie *m*

talent /'tælənt, 'talənt/ • *n* talent
m

talk /tɔːk, tɔk/ • *n* samtale *m*;
foredrag *n*, forelesning *f*; prat
n, snakk *n* • *v* snakke, preke

tank /tæŋk/ ; stridsvogn, tanks

tap /tæp/ • *n* tappekran *m*; kran
m • *v* tappe; avlytte

target /'tɑɪgɪt, tɑːgɪt/ • *n*
skyteskive

taste /teɪst/ • *n* smak *m*;
smakebit *m* • *v* smake

taught *(sp/pp)* ▷ TEACH

tax /tæks/ • *n* skatt, avgift • *v*
skattelegge

taxi /'tæk.si/ • *v* takse

tea /ti, tiː/ • *n* te

teach /tiːtʃ/ • *v* (*sp* taught, *pp*
taught) undervise, lære

team /tiːm/ • *n* spann *n*

tear /tɛə, tɛɚ/ • *n* tårer

technical /'tɛk.nɪk.əl/ • *adj*
teknisk **~ly** • *adv* Teknisk sett;
teknisk

technolog|y /tɛkˈnɒlədʒi,
tɛkˈnɑlədʒi/ • *n* teknologi *f*

teeth *(pl)* ▷ TOOTH

telephone /'tɛlɪfəʊn, 'tɛləfoʊn/ • *n*
telefon *m*

tell /tɛl/ • *v* (*sp* told, *pp* told)
fortelle

tempt /tɛmpt/ • *v* friste

ten /tɛn, tɪn/ • *num* ti

tenant /'tɛ.nənt/ ; leieboer

tendency /'tɛndənsi/ • *n* tendens
m

~ion • *n* spenning

term /tɜːm, tɜːm/ • *n* vilkår *n*

terrible /'tɛ.rə.b̩/ • *adv* fryktelig,
forferdelig; ubehagelig

text /tɛkst/ • *n* tekst

than /ðæn, ðən/ • *prep* enn

thank /θæŋk/ • *v* takke **~s** •
interj takk

Thanksgiving • *n* thanksgiving
m

that /'ðæt, 'ðɛt/ • *conj* at • *pron*
(*pl* those) som

the /ðiː, ði/ • *art* -en

theat|er /'θi(ə)tɚ, 'θi.eɪ.tɚ/ • *n*
teater *n*

theatre *(British)* ▷ THEATER

them /ðɛm, ðəm/ • *pron* dem

then /ðɛn, ðən/ • *adv* da, den
gang; så, deretter, siden; i så
fall

theology /θi.ˈɒ.lə.dʒi/ • *n* teologi

theor|y /'θɪəɹi, 'θi:əɹi/ • *n* teori *m*

there /ðɛə(ɹ), ðɛɚ/ • *adv* der; dit

these /ðiːz, ðiz/ • *det* disse

thesis /'θiːsɪs/ • *n* tese *m*

they /ðeɪ/ • *pron* de

thigh /θaɪ/ • *n* lår *n*

thin /θɪn/ • *adj* tynn; smal; slank

T

thing /θɪŋ/ • *n* ting *m*, dings *m*, greie *f*

think /θɪŋk/ • *v* tenke, fundere; resonnere; komme på; synes, mene; tro, anta

thirst /θɜːst, θɜ̃st/ • *n* tørste **~y** • *adj* tørst

thirteen /ˈθɜː.tiːn, ˈθɜ̃(t).tin/ • *num* tretten

this /ðɪs/ • *pron* (*pl* these) denne *f*, dette *n*

thorough /ˈθʌ.ɹə, ˈθʌ.ɹoʊ/ ; grundig, nøyaktig, nøye

those /ðəʊz, ðoʊz/ • *det* de

though /ðəʊ, ðoʊ/ • *conj* selv om

thousand /ˈθaʊz(ə)nd/ • *num* tusen

thread /θɹɛd/ • *n* tråd *m*

three /θɹiː, θɹi/ • *num* tre, tri

threshold /ˈθɹɛʃ(h)əʊld, ˈθɹɛʃ(h)ould/ ; terskel *m*

threw *(sp)* ▷ THROW

thrive /θɹaɪv/ • *v* blomstre

throat /θɹəʊt, θɹoʊt/ • *n* hals *m*; svelg *n*

through /θɹuː, θɹu/ • *prep* gjennom; ved at; gjennom at

throw /θɹəʊ, θɹoʊ/ • *n* kast *n*; teppe *n* • *v* (*sp* threw, *pp* thrown) kaste, hive **~ sth away** • *v* kaste

thrown *(pp)* ▷ THROW

thrust /θɹʌst/ • *v* (*sp* thrust, *pp* thrust) støt

thumb /θʌm/ ; tommeskrue *m*

thunder /ˈθʌndə, ˈθʌndɚ/ • *v* tordne

Thursday • *n* torsdag

thus /ðʌs/ • *adv* sånn, slik, på denne måten

tick /tɪk/ • *n* flått *m*

ticket /ˈtɪkɪt/ ; bot *f*

tight /taɪt/ • *adj* snever

till /tɪl/ • *prep* til, inntil

timber /ˈtɪmbə, ˈtɪmbɚ/ • *n* tømmer *n*; trevirke *n*; takbjelke *m*

time /taɪm, tɑem/ • *n* tid *f*; tempo; soningstid *f*, tid inne; gang *m* • *v* ta tid

tin /tɪn/ • *n* tinn

tir|e /ˈtaɪə(ɹ), ˈtaɪɚ/ • *v* bli trett **~ing** • *adj* slitsom

tit /tɪt/ • *n* pupp *m*

title /ˈtaɪtl/ ; overskrift

to /tuː, tu/ ; til

tobacco /təˈbækoʊ/ • *n* tobakk

today /təˈdeɪ/ • *adv* idag • *n* i dag

toe /təʊ, toʊ/ • *n* tå

together /tʊˈɡɛð.ə(ɹ), tʊˈɡɛðɚ/ • *adv* i lag; samlet

toilet /ˈtɔɪ.lət/ • *n* pynting; omkledningsrom *n*; toalett *n*, vannklosett *n*; dass *n*

Tokyo • *n* Tokyo

told *(sp/pp)* ▷ TELL

tolera|te /ˈtɑl.ə.ɹaɪ, ˈtɒl.ə.ɹeɪt/ • *v* tolerere, tåle

tomorrow /təˈmɒɹəʊ, təˈmɒɹoʊ/ • *n* i morgen *m*

tone /təʊn, toʊn/ • *n* tone

tongue /tʌŋ, tɒŋ/ • *n* pløse *f*; tunge

tonight /təˈnait/ • *n* i kveld, i natt

too /tuː, tu/ ; for, altfor

took *(sp)* ▷ TAKE

tool /tuːl/ • *n* verktøy *n*; kuk *m* • *v* bearbeide; utstyre utruste

tooth /tuːθ, tuθ/ ; tann

tore *(sp)* ▷ TEAR

torn *(pp)* ▷ TEAR

T

torture /ˈtɔːtʃə, ˈtɔːˈtʃə(r)/ • *n*
tortur *m* • *v* torturere

toss /tɒs, tɔs/ ; flipp *n*, kast *n*,
myntkast *n*; flippe, kaste

touch /tʌtʃ/ • *n* følelse *m*; kontakt
m; berøre, røre

touris|t /ˈtʊərɪst, ˈtɔːrɪst/ • *n* turist
~m • *n* turisme

toward /təˈwɔːd, tʊˈwɔːd/ • *prep*
mot; angående; på grunn av

trace /treɪs/ • *n* kretskort *n*

trade /treɪd/ ; handel *m*;
håndverk *n*, fag *n* **~mark** • *n*
varemerke

traffic /ˈtræfɪk/ • *n* trafikk *m*,
ferdsel

train /treɪn/ • *n* tog *n* • *v* trene,
øve; mosjonere

trait /treɪ, treɪt/ • *n* trekk *n*

transit /ˈtrænzɪt, ˈtrænzət/ • *n*
passasje **~ion** • *n* overgang *m*

translat|e /trɑːnzˈleɪt, ˈtrænzleɪt/ •
v oversette

transparent /træn(t)sˈpærənt,
træn(t)sˈpɛrənt/ • *adj*
gjennomsiktig, transparent;
gjennomsynlig,
gjennomskuelig; opplagt,
åpenbar

transport /ˈtrænzpɔːt, trænzˈpɔːt/
• *v* føre

trap /træp/ • *n* felle

trash /træʃ/ • *n* avfall *n*, søppel
n, boss *n*

travel /ˈtrævəl/ ; slaglengde *m* • *v*
reise *m*

treasure /ˈtrɛʒə, ˈtrɛʒə/ • *n* skatt
m

treat /triːt/ • *n* påspandering • *v*
behandle; påspandere

treaty /ˈtriːti, ˈtriːdi/ • *n* traktat *m*

tree /triː, trɪ/ • *n* tre *n*

trick /trɪk/ • *n* trick *n*, trikk *n*,
triks *n*, knep *n*; stikk *n*;
horekunde *m* • *v* lure, narre

trip /trɪp/ • *v* reise

triple /ˈtrɪpəl/ • *v* tredoble

troop /truːp/ • *n* tropp *f*

true /truː, trɪu/ • *adj* sann; tro,
trofast; ekte

trust /trʌst/ • *n* kredittverdighet
m; til å stole på, pålitelig; tillit
m; forhåpning *m* • *v* ha tillit;
være trygg; stole på, ha tillit
til; tro på

try /traɪ/ • *v* prøve, forsøke; stille
for retten **~ sth out** • *v*
utprøve

Tuesday • *n* tirsdag

Turk|ey /ˈtɜːki, ˈtɜːki/ • *n* Tyrkia

turn /tɜːn, tɜn/ • *n* sving,
vending, vridning; omdreining;
etter tur; tur *m* • *v* endre,
forvandle; dreie; snu, snurre;
skru; tørne; vende; svinge; bli
~ sth off • *v* slått på, skru av,
få av **~ sth on** • *v* slå på, skru på
in ~ • *phr* deretter; i tur

turnover • *n* omsetning *f*

Tuvalu • *n* Tuvalu

TV • *n* TV, teve

twelve /twɛlv/ • *num* tolv

twent|y /ˈtwɛnti, ˈtwʌnti/ • *num*
tjue, tyve **~ieth** • *adj* tjuende

twist /twɪst/ • *v* vri

two /tuː, tu/ • *num* to
~writer • *n* skrivemaskin *m*

UAE *(abbr)* ▷ UNITED ARAB
EMIRATES
ugly /ˈʌgli/ • *adj* stygg,
frastøtende; ekkel, vemmelig;
vond
uh /ʌː/ • *interj* eh, øh
UK *(abbr)* ▷ UNITED KINGDOM
Ukrain|e • *n* Ukraina
ultimate /ˈʌltɪmɪt, ˈʌltəmɪt/ • *adj*
endelig; ultimat
umbrella /ʌmˈbrɛlə/ ; paraply *m*
under /ˈʌndə(ɹ), ˈʌndɚ/ • *prep*
under
underground • *adj* underjordisk
understand /(ˌ)ʌndəˈstænd,
ˌʌndɚˈstænd/ • *v* forstå,
skjønne, kunne; fatte
unfortunate /ʌnˈfɔːtʃʊnət,
ʌnˈfɔrtʃʊnət/ • *adj* uheldig
union /ˈjuːnjən/ ; union *m*
unique /juːˈniːk, juˈniːk/ • *adj* unik
universe /ˈjuːnɪˌvɜːs, ˈjuːnəˌvɜs/ • *n*
univers *n*
unless /ənˈlɛs/ • *conj* hvis ikke
unlike /ʌnˈlaɪk/ • *adj* ulik
unnecessary /ʌnˈnɛsəsəs(ə)ɹɪ,
ʌnˈnɛsəˌsɛɹɪ/ • *adj* unødvendig
unveil /ʌnˈveɪl/ • *v* avdekke;
blottstille
up /ʌp, ap/ • *adj* i tur; opp; oppe;
med, oppdatert; utgående;
ute; oppesen; klar; med …
opp • *adv* opp • *prep* oppover
• *v* høyne, øke; forfremme

update /ˈʌp.deɪt, əpˈdeɪt/ • *n*
ajourføring, oppdatering • *v*
oppdatere
upgrade /ˈʌp.ɡɹeɪd, əpˈɡɹeɪd/ • *v*
oppgrade
upon /əˈpɒn, əˈpɑn/ • *prep* oppå;
på; ved
upper /ˈʌpə, ˈʌpɚ/ • *adj* øvre
urge /ɜːdʒ, ɜdʒ/ • *n* trang *m*
us /ʌs, əs/ • *pron* oss
USA *(abbr)* ▷ UNITED STATES
us|e /juːs, juːz/ ; nytte *m* • *v* bruke
~eful • *adj* nyttig **~eless** • *adj*
nytteløs, unyttig **~er**; bruker
~ed to • *adj* ha for vane **~age**
• *n* bruksområde *n*;
anvendelse *m*; bruk *m*
~ly • *adv* vanligvis
Uzbekistan • *n* Usbekistan

vacation /vəˈkeɪʃ(ə)n, veɪˈkeɪʃən/ •
n ferie *m*
~ation • *n* vaksinering *f*
value /ˈvæljuː, ˈvælju/ • *n* verd *n*,
verdi *m*; betydning; pris *m* • *v*
verdsette, taksere; vurdere;
skatte; sette pris på
Vanuatu • *n* Vanuatu
vari|able /ˈvɛəɹɪ.ə.bl̩, ˈvæɹ.i.ə.bl̩/ •
adj variabel; varierende;
avvikende • *n* variabel *m*
~ous • *adj* ymse, ulike
vast /vɑːst, væst/ • *adj* enorm,
voldsom

verb /vɜːb, vɜːb/ ● *n* verb
verse /vɜːs, ˈvɜːs/ ● *n* vers *n*
version /ˈvɜːʒən, ˈvɜːʒən/ ● *n* versjon
versus /ˈvɜːsəs, ˈvɜːsəs/ ● *prep* versus
very /ˈvɛɹi/ ● *adj* samme; veldig, aller
victim /ˈvɪktɪm, ˈvɪktəm/ ● *n* offer *n*
view /vjuː/ ● *n* utsyn *n*, utsikt *m*, sikt *m*; syn *n*; synspunkt *n*; visning *m* ● *v* se på
vigilant /ˈvɪdʒɪlənt/ ● *adj* oppmerksom, forsiktig
village /ˈvɪlɪdʒ/ ● *n* landsby, torp *n*
virtue /ˈvɜːˌtjuː/ ● *n* dyd *m*
visa /ˈviːzə/ ● *n* visum
visible /ˈvɪzəb(ə)l/ ● *adj* synlig
~ion ● *n* åpenbaring *f*
vital /ˈvaɪtəl, ˈvaɪtəl/ ● *adj* vital, livsviktig; livsoppholdende; levende; kjempeviktig
vocal /ˈvəʊkəl, ˈvoʊkəl/ ● *adj* vokal *m*; vokale *f*
volcano /vɒlˈkeɪnəʊ, vɑlˈkeɪnoʊ/ ● *n* vulkan *m*
vote /vəʊt, voʊt/ ● *v* stemme
vulture /ˈvʌltʃə, ˈvʌltʃɚ/ ● *n* gribb *m*

W

wagon /ˈwæg(ə)n, ˈwægən/ ● *n* vogn *f*

waist /weɪst/ ● *n* midje
~ing ● *n* vente
waiter /ˈweɪtə, ˈweɪtɚ/ ; ventende *m*
wake /weɪk/ ● *v* (*sp* woke, *pp* woken) vekke **~ up** ● *v* våkne
waked (*sp/pp*) ▷ WAKE
walk /wɔːk, wɔk/ ● *v* gå, spasere; slippe løs; vandre; gå på tur med, gå ut med hunden
wall /wɔːl, wɔl/ ● *n* voll *m*; forhindring *m*; skillevegg *m*
want /wɒnt, wɑnt/ ● *n* mangel; behov ● *v* ville, ønske
war /wɔː, wɔɹ/ ● *n* krig *m*
ward /wɔːd, wɔɹd/ ; menighet
warm /wɔːm, wɔɹm/ ● *adj* varm
warn /wɔːn, wɔɹn/ ● *v* advare
warrant /ˈwɒɹənt, ˈwɔɹənt/ ● *v* garantere, forsikre
was (*sp*) ▷ BE
wash /wɒʃ, wɔʃ/ ● *v* tvette, vaske
watch /wɒtʃ, wɔtʃ/ ● *n* vakt; klokke, ur ● *v* passe på; observere, se på
water /ˈwɔːtə, ˈwɒtə/ ● *n* vann *m*; tiss *n*; drikkevann ● *v* gråte, felle tårer; tisse
wave /weɪv/ ; vinke
way /weɪ/ ; måte **by the ~** ● *phr* forresten
weave /wiːv/ ● *n* vev *f* ● *v* (*sp* wove, *pp* woven) veve; spinne; kjøre sikksakk, traversere, sno seg gjennom
wed /wɛd/ ● *v* (*sp* wed, *pp* wed) vie, ektevie; ekte, gifte seg med
wedded (*sp/pp*) ▷ WED
weed /wiːd/ ● *n* ugress *n*; hasj, pot

welcome /'wɛlkəm/ • *n* velkomst *m*

well /wɛl/ • *adv* bra • *n* brønn

went *(sp)* ▷ GO

wept *(sp/pp)* ▷ WEEP

were *(sp)* ▷ BE

~ern; vestlig • *n* western *m*

wet /wɛt/ • *adj* våt, fuktig; bløt; vått

wetted *(sp/pp)* ▷ WET

what /wɔt, ʍɒt/ ; hva

whatever /ʍɒt'ɛvə, ʍʌt'ɛvəʳ/ • *interj* samma det!, whatever!

~chair • *n* rullestol *m*

when /ʍɛn, ʍɪn/ • *adv* når; da • *pron* når

where /ʍɛə(ɹ), ʍɛəʳ/ • *conj* hvor

~by • *adv* hvorved **~ver** • *conj* hvor enn

whether /'wɛðə(ɹ), 'ʍɛðə(ɹ)/ • *conj* om

which /wɪtʃ, ʍɪtʃ/ • *pron* som

while /ʍaɪl/ • *n* stund *m*

whine /waɪn, ʍaɪn/ • *n* hvin *n*, hyl *n* • *v* hvine, hyle; sutre, syte, jamre

whip /wɪp, ʍɪp/ • *n* pisk

whiskey /'wɪski, 'ʍɪski/ • *n* whisky

whistle /'wɪsl̩/ • *v* plystre

who /huː/ • *pron* hvem **~se** • *det* hvem sin, hvems, hvis

whole /həʊl, hoʊl/ • *adj* hel • *adv* helt • *n* helhet *m*

why /ʍaɪ/ • *interj* hvorfor • *n* derfor

wid|e /waɪd, wɑɪd/ • *adv* vidt, bredt; vid

wild /waɪld/ • *adj* vill

will /wɪl/ • *n* vilje *m*, ønske *n*; testament *n* • *v* vil, kommer til å, skal; testamentere; ville

win /wɪn/ • *n* seier *m* • *v* *(sp* won, *pp* won) vinne; overvinne

wind /wɪnd, waɪnd/ • *n* vind *m*; fjert *m*, fis *m*, promp *m*

wine /waɪn/ • *n* vin

winter /'wɪntə, 'wɪntəʳ/ • *v* overvintre

wipe /waɪp/ • *v* tørke av, viske; slette

wire /waɪə(ɹ), 'waɪəʳ/ • *v* overføre

wis|e /waɪz/ • *adj* vis **~dom** • *n* visdom *m*

wit /wɪt/ • *n* vett *n*; forstand *m*, intellekt *n*; vidd *n* **~ty** • *adj* vittig, åndrik

~in; innenfor; innen

witness /'wɪtnəs/ • *n* vitne *n*

wives *(pl)* ▷ WIFE

woke *(sp)* ▷ WAKE

woken *(pp)* ▷ WAKE

women *(pl)* ▷ WOMAN

won *(sp/pp)* ▷ WIN

wonder /'wʌndə, 'wʌndəʳ/ • *v* undres **~ful** • *adj* underfull

wood /wʊd/ • *n* tre *n*, treverk *n*, ved; treslag *n*, tresort *m* **~pecker** • *n* hakkespett *m*

word /wɜːd, wɝd/ • *n* ord *n*; lovnad *m*; krangel *m*

wore *(sp)* ▷ WEAR

work /wɜːk, wɝk/ • *n* arbeid *n*, jobb, verk *n* • *v* arbeide, jobbe; fungere, virke, gå **~out** • *n* treningsøkt **~shop** • *n* verksted

world /wɜːld, wɝld/ ; verden *m*

W

worm /wɜːm, wɜ̃m/ • *n* mark *m*, makk *m*, orm *m* • *v* krype, kravle, åle

worn *(pp)* ▷ WEAR

worr|y /ˈwʌɹi, ˈwʊɹi/ ; uroe • *(also)* ▷ GOOD

~while • *adj* umaken verd

wound /wuːnd, wund/ • *n* sår *n*, skade *m* • *v* skade; såre • *(also)* ▷ WIND

wove *(sp)* ▷ WEAVE

woven *(pp)* ▷ WEAVE

wreck /ˈɹɛk/ • *n* vrak *n*

wren /ɹɛn/ • *n* gjerdesmett *m*

wrinkle • *n* rynke

writ|e /ɹaɪt/ • *v* (*sp* wrote, *pp* written) skrive **~er** • *n* forfatter *m*, skribent *m*

wrong /ɹɒŋ, ɹɔŋ/ • *adj* galt, uriktig; gal; feil; vrang • *adv* galt

wrote *(sp)* ▷ WRITE

wrung *(sp/pp)* ▷ WRING

yard /jɑːd, jɑɪd/ • *n* gård; yard *m*

yeah /jɛə̯/ • *part* ja, yeah

yeast /jiːst, iːst/ • *n* gjær *m*

yell /jɛl/ • *v* rope, skrike

yellow /ˈjɛl.əʊ, ˈjɛl.oʊ/ • *adj* gul

yes /jɛs/ • *interj* yes *n* • *part* ja; jo

yet /jɛt/ • *adv* ennå, enda

yield /jiːld/ • *v* svikte, gi etter; yte; multiplisere; resultere i

you /juː, ju/ • *det* din

young /jʌŋ/ • *adj* ung

your /jɔː, jɔːɹ/ • *det* din *m*, di *f*, ditt *n*, dine

youth /juːθ, juθ/ • *n* ungdom *m*; yngling

zeal /ziːl/ • *n* engasjement *n*, iver *m* **~ous** • *adj* engasjert, ivrig, nidkjær, flittig

zero /ˈzɪəɹəʊ, ˈzɪɹ(ˌ)oʊ/ ; nullpunkt *n*; null *n*

Norwegian-English

A

abnorm • *adj* abnormal
abolisjon • *n* abolition
abort • *n* abortion
absolutt • *adj* absolute
absorbere • *v* absorb
abstraksjon • *n* abstract
abstrakt • *adj* abstract
addere • *v* add
addisjon • *n* addition
adekvat • *adj* adequate
adjø • *interj* bye, goodbye
adlyde • *v* obey
adresse • *n* address
advare • *v* warn
advarsel • *n* alert
affekt • *n* affect
affektere • *v* affect
Afghanistan • *n* Afghanistan

afrikansk • *adj* African
aften • *n* night
agenda • *n* agenda
agent • *n* agent
aggressiv • *adj* aggressive
ai • *interj* oh
AIDS • *n* AIDS
ajourføring • *n* update
akademi • *n* academy
akademiker • *n* academic
akademisk • *adj* academic
akkar • *n* squid
akselerere • *v* accelerate
aksent • *n* accent
aksentuere • *v* accent
aksepetere • *v* accept
akseptere • *v* accept
aksess • *n* access
aksessere • *v* access
aksje • *n* equity, share, stake
aksjeeier • *n* shareholder
aksjonær • *n* shareholder
aktelse • *n* regard
akterende • *n* stern

aktiv ● *adj* active
aktuell ● *adj* current
alarm ● *n* alert
aldri ● *adv* never
alene ● *adv* alone
Algerie ● *n* Algeria
alibi ● *n* alibi
alle ● *det* all, each ● *pron* everybody
allé ● *n* alley
aller ● *adv* very
allerede ● *adv* already
allmenn ● *adj* general, public
allmennt ● *adj* public
allminnelig ● *adj* general
alltid ● *adv* always
allting ● *pron* everything
alminnelig ● *adj* normal
alt ● *n* all ● *det* each ● *pron* everything
alternativ ● *adj* alternative
altfor ● *adv* too
alvorlig ● *adj* important, serious
ambassade ● *n* embassy
amme ● *v* breastfeed
Amsterdam ● *n* Amsterdam
analyse ● *n* analysis
anbefale ● *v* encourage
anbringe ● *v* pose
andel ● *n* fraction
andpusten ● *phr* out of breath
andre ● *adj* other, second
anfall ● *n* access
angivelig ● *adv* allegedly
Angola ● *n* Angola
angrep ● *n* attempt, charge
angriper ● *n* attacker
angst ● *n* anxiety
angå ● *v* concern
angående ● *prep* about, toward
anklagede ● *n* defendant

ankomme ● *v* arrive, come
ankomst ● *n* entrance
anmeldelse ● *n* review
annektere ● *v* appropriate
annen ● *adj* other
annonse ● *n* commercial
anormal ● *adj* abnormal
anseelse ● *n* face
ansette ● *v* employ, hire
ansikt ● *n* face
anskaffe ● *v* purchase
anskaffelse ● *n* purchase
anslag ● *adj* hit
ansvar ● *n* burden, responsibility
anta ● *v* suppose, think
antakelig ● *adj* acceptable
antyde ● *v* hint
anvendelse ● *n* usage
anvise ● *v* indicate
appelsin ● *n* orange
appelsintre ● *n* orange
appetitt ● *n* appetite
applikasjon ● *n* application
arabisk ● *adj* Arab
arbeid ● *n* job, work
arbeide ● *v* work
arbeidsky ● *adj* indolent
arbeidsrom ● *n* study
Argentina ● *n* Argentina
argumentere ● *v* dispute
ark ● *n* leaf, paper
arkitektur ● *n* architecture
arkiv ● *n* file
arkivere ● *v* file
arm ● *n* arm
armatur ● *n* frame
arr ● *n* scar
arrogant ● *adj* arrogant
artig ● *adj* funny
artikkel ● *n* article, paper

A
B

artikulasjon • *n* articulation
arv • *n* heritage, legacy
arve • *v* inherit
arving • *n* heir
asen • *n* ass
Asia • *n* Asia
asiat • *n* Asian
ask • *n* ash
astronomi • *n* astronomy
asyl • *n* asylum
at • *conj* that
atlet • *n* athlete
atten • *num* eighteen
attmed • *prep* next
attraktiv • *adj* attractive
attributt • *n* attribute
auksjon • *n* sale
Australia • *n* Australia
australsk • *adj* Australian
automatisk • *adj* automatic
av • *prep* by, of • *adj* off • *adv* out
avbryte • *v* interrupt, suspend
avdekke • *v* unveil
avfall • *n* garbage, trash
avfyre • *v* fire
avføring • *n* shit
avgift • *n* duty, tax
avhengighet • *n* addiction
avhøra • *v* interrogate
avispapir • *n* newspaper
avkjøle • *v* chill
avkrysse • *v* check
avling • *n* harvest
avlytte • *v* tap
avskaffe • *v* abolish
avskjed • *interj* goodbye
avskjedige • *v* fire
avskrekke • *v* deter
avskrive • *v* abandon
avslutning • *n* finish

avslutte • *v* close, end, finish
avsløre • *v* reveal
avslå • *v* decline, reject
avsnitt • *n* paragraph
avsondre • *v* separate
avstemming • *n* reconciliation
avtale • *n* agreement
avtrykk • *n* print
avvente • *v* halt
avvik • *n* departure
avvikende • *adj* variable
avvise • *v* decline, reject

back • *n* back
bad • *n* bath, bathroom
bade • *n* bath
badekar • *n* bath
baderom • *n* bathroom
bagge • *v* bag
Bahamas • *n* Bahamas
Bahrain • *n* Bahrain
bak • *prep* after, behind • *n* back, butt, can
bakende • *n* back
bakeri • *n* bakery
bakke • *n* ground, slope
bakpart • *n* behind
bakrus • *n* hangover
bakside • *n* back
balanse • *n* balance
balansere • *v* balance
ball • *n* nut
ballong • *n* balloon
balltre • *n* bat

ballveksling • *n* rally
banal • *adj* light
banan • *n* banana
bananplante • *n* banana
band • *n* band
bande • *n* band
bane • *n* course, field
Bangladesh • *n* Bangladesh
bank • *n* bank
banke • *n* bank, bed • *v* knock
bankerott • *v* bankrupt
banner • *n* banner
bar • *n* bar
Barbados • *n* Barbados
bare • *adv* alone, only, solely
barmhjertighet • *n* mercy
barn • *n* child, infant, kid
barndomshjem • *n* home
bass • *n* bass
batteri • *n* pile
batterist • *n* drummer
baug • *n* forward
be • *v* pray
bearbeide • *v* tool
beboer • *n* resident
bebyrde • *v* charge
bed • *n* bed
bedra • *v* cheat
bedrageri • *n* fraud
bedre • *adv* better
befalingsmand • *n* commander
befeste • *v* consolidate
befolkning • *n* folk
befri • *v* deliver, free
begavet • *adj* clever
begeistring • *n* enthusiasm
begravelse • *n* funeral
begrensning • *n* limit
begrep • *n* concept
begripe • *v* grasp

begynne • *v* begin, commence, start
behage • *v* please
behagelig • *adj* agreeable
behandle • *v* treat
behendig • *adj* agile
beherske • *v* master
behersket • *adj* cool
beholde • *v* keep
beholder • *n* container
behov • *n* demand, want
Beijing • *n* Beijing
bein • *n* leg
beingrind • *n* frame
bek • *n* pitch
bekjempe • *v* fight
bekjentgjøre • *v* disclose
bekjentgørelse • *n* announcement
bekk • *n* burn
beklage • *v* apologize
beklagelse • *n* regret
bekledning • *n* clothes
bekrefte • *v* confirm
bekvemmelighet • *adj* expedient
bekymring • *n* concern
belaste • *v* charge
belastning • *n* burden
Belize • *n* Belize
belte • *n* belt
belyst • *adj* light
belønning • *n* reward
bemanne • *v* man
bemerke • *v* notice
bemyndige • *v* authorize, empower
bend • *n* elbow
benektelse • *n* denial
benevning • *n* designation
Benin • *n* Benin

B

benk • *n* bench
benke • *v* bench
bensin • *n* gasoline
beredt • *adj* ready
bergart • *n* rock
bergmynte • *n* oregano
beryktet • *adj* infamous
berømt • *adj* famous, renowned
berøre • *v* touch
beseire • *v* defeat
besette • *v* occupy
beskjeden • *adj* humble
beskyldning • *n* charge
beskytte • *v* defend, protect
best • *adj* best • *n* best
bestandig • *adv* always
beste • *n* best
bestemme • *v* set
bestemor • *n* grandmother
bestemt • *adj* particular
bestige • *v* mount
bestille • *v* book, order, reserve
bestilling • *n* reserve
bestå • *v* exist
besvergelse • *n* spell
besøksrett • *n* access
betale • *v* foot
betalingsutsettelse • *n* grace
betegnelse • *n* designation
betinge • *v* condition
betone • *v* highlight
betoning • *n* accent
betrakte • *v* consider
betraktning • *n* regard
bety • *v* mean
betydelig • *adj* important
betydning • *n* meaning, value
beundring • *n* admiration
bevare • *v* husband, keep, maintain
bevegelig • *adj* mobile

bevegelse • *n* movement
bevegelseshemmet • *adj* disabled
bevis • *n* evidence
bevise • *v* evidence
bevismateriale • *n* evidence
bevissthet • *n* consciousness, mind
bevokte • *v* guard
Bhutan • *n* Bhutan
bibel • *n* Bible
bibliotek • *n* library
bibliotekar • *n* librarian
bidra • *v* contribute
bie • *n* bee
bikkje • *n* dog
bikube • *n* beehive
bilde • *n* picture
bilgummi • *n* rubber
bille • *n* beetle
billettpris • *n* fare
bind • *n* band
binde • *v* band, bind
bindeord • *n* conjunction
bistand • *n* support
bit • *n* bit
bite • *v* bite
biting • *n* bite
bitt • *n* bit, bite
bitter • *adj* bitter
bjelkelag • *n* frame
blad • *n* blade, leaf
blakk • *adj* broke, poor
blande • *v* confuse, mix
blank • *adj* blank
blant • *prep* among
bleik • *adj* pale
blek • *adj* light, pale
blekne • *v* pale
blende • *v* blind
blessa • *v* bless

bli • *v* get, stay, turn
blinde • *v* blind
blink • *n* lightning
blodprøve • *n* blood
blodsbånd • *n* blood
blokk • *n* block, pad
blomstre • *v* thrive
blond • *adj* blond
blondine • *n* blond
blottstille • *v* unveil
bly • *n* lead
blyant • *n* pencil
blø • *v* bleed
bløt • *adj* soft, wet
bløtgjøre • *v* soften
blå • *adj* blue
blåfarge • *n* blue
blåkopi • *n* carbon
blåne • *n* horizon
blåpapir • *n* carbon
bo • *v* live
bokettersyn • *n* audit
boks • *n* box, can
bolig • *n* residence
Bolivia • *n* Bolivia
bom • *n* bar
bombe • *n* bomb
bondefangeri • *n* scam
bondsk • *adj* churlish
boområder • *n* neighborhood
bor • *n* drill
bord • *n* board, border, table
borde • *v* board
bordsalt • *n* salt
bore • *v* drill
borg • *n* castle
borger • *n* citizen
borgtårn • *n* keep
bornert • *adj* narrow-minded
borte • *adv* out
bortenfor • *prep* past

bortgang • *n* departure
boss • *n* boss, garbage, trash
bot • *n* fine, ticket
Botswana • *n* Botswana
bra • *adj* fine • *adv* well
bragd • *n* exploit
brann • *n* fire
Brasil • *n* Brazil
bratt • *adj* steep
bredt • *adv* wide
brems • *n* brake
bremse • *v* halt
brenne • *v* burn, fire
brennemerke • *v* brand
brenning • *n* burn
brennmerke • *n* brand
brett • *n* plate
briller • *n* spectacles
brilleseddel • *n* prescription
bringe • *n* breast • *v* take
brodd • *n* stinger
brok • *n* pants
bronse • *n* bronze
bronsefarge • *n* bronze
bronsefarget • *adj* bronze
bronsere • *v* bronze
bror • *n* brother
brors • *v* brother
brorskap • *n* brotherhood
bruk • *n* usage
bruke • *v* spend, use
bruker • *n* user
bruksområde • *n* usage
brun • *n* brown
Brunei • *n* Brunei
brunst • *n* heat, pride
bry • *n* bother • *v* mind
bryllupsdag • *n* anniversary
brysom • *v* annoying
bryst • *n* breast, chest
brystkasse • *n* chest

brød • *n* bread
brøk • *n* fraction
brøkdel • *n* fraction
brønn • *n* well
bu • *n* booth
bubla • *n* bubble
buk • *n* stomach
bukk • *n* horse
bukse • *n* pants
bukt • *n* bay
Bulgaria • *n* Bulgaria
bunke • *n* bunch
bunn • *n* bed
bur • *n* cage
burde • *v* should
Burma • *n* Myanmar
burugle • *n* bag
Burundi • *n* Burundi
busk • *n* bush
buskap • *n* cattle
buss • *n* bus
busse • *v* bus
butikk • *n* shop
by • *n* city
bydel • *n* quarter
bygge • *n* building
bygning • *n* building
byrde • *n* burden, charge, imposition
byregion • *n* metropolitan
byråkrati • *n* bureaucracy
bære • *v* bear
bærekraftig • *adj* sustainable
bæsj • *n* shit
bæsje • *v* shit
bøg • *adj* gay
bøling • *n* cattle
bønne • *n* bean
bønnemøte • *n* prayer
bøtelegge • *v* fine
bøye • *v* bend

bøylesaks • *n* shear
bål • *n* fire
bånd • *n* band

cancer • *n* cancer
chat • *n* chat
chatte • *v* chat
Chile • *n* Chile
chille • *v* chill
chips • *n* chip
Colombia • *n* Colombia
cool • *adj* cool
crack • *n* rock
cruise • *n* cruise
Cuba • *n* Cuba

da • *conj* as, since, when • *adv* then
daddel • *n* date
daffe • *v* drift
dag • *n* day
dagbok • *n* diary, journal
dagligvarebutikk • *n* grocery
dama • *n* queen
dame • *n* lady, queen
dammen • *n* pond
Danmark • *n* Denmark
dass • *n* toilet

dataminne • *n* memory
datamus • *n* mouse
date • *n* date • *v* go
datere • *v* date
datering • *n* date
datert • *adj* dated
datter • *n* daughter
datterdatter • *n* granddaughter
de • *pron* they • *det* those
deaktivert • *adj* off
debatt • *n* contest, debate, discussion
decennium • *n* decade
dedikere • *v* dedicate
definisjonsområde • *n* domain
definitivt • *adv* definitely
deilig • *adj* fit
dekade • *n* decade
dekk • *n* rubber
dekke • *v* comprehend, lay, protect, set
del • *n* part
dele • *v* divide, part, share
delegere • *v* delegate
delta • *v* participate
dem • *pron* them
demokrati • *n* democracy
dempe • *v* mute
den • *pron* it
denne • *pron* this
dens • *det* its
deplasement • *n* displacement
depositum • *n* deposit
deprimert • *adj* depressed
der • *adv* there
derav • *adv* hence
dereliksjon • *n* abandonment
deretter • *adv* accordingly, then • *phr* in turn
derfor • *adv* hence • *n* why
derpå • *adv* afterwards

desennium • *n* decade
dessert • *n* dessert
destillasjonsapparat • *n* still
det • *pron* it
dets • *det* its
dette • *pron* this
di • *det* your
dialog • *n* dialogue
diamant • *n* diamond
differensiering • *n* differentiation
digge • *v* dig
dikkedal • *n* dolphin
dikt • *n* poem
dilemma • *n* fix
dimensjon • *n* dimension
din • *det* you, your
dine • *det* your
dings • *n* thing
direkt • *adj* direct
direkte • *adj* forward • *adv* live
direktør • *n* director
dirk • *n* pick
disciplinere • *v* discipline
diskresjon • *n* discretion
diskusjon • *n* contest, discussion
diskutere • *v* discuss, dispute
disputt • *n* dispute
disse • *det* these
distinksjon • *n* distinction
distrahere • *v* distract
distrahert • *adj* abstract
distraksjon • *n* abstract
dit • *adv* there
ditt • *det* your
dividere • *v* divide
djevel • *n* devil
djevelsk • *adj* devilish
do • *n* can
dokumentar • *n* documentary

dollar • *n* dollar
dom • *n* sentence
domstol • *n* court
donasjon • *n* grant
doven • *adj* flat
dra • *v* go, part, pull
drag • *n* allure, gasp
drap • *n* kill
drapsmann • *n* killer
dreie • *v* turn
drepe • *v* kill, murder
drikke • *v* drink
drikkevann • *n* water
drikking • *n* drinking
drill • *n* drill
drille • *v* drill
dristig • *adj* saucy
drita • *adj* drunk
dritt • *n* mute, shit
drive • *v* chase, drive • *phr* at home
dronning • *n* queen
drukne • *v* drown
drøfte • *v* negotiate
drømme • *v* dream
dugg • *n* fog
dugge • *v* fog
dum • *adj* dull, stupid
dumskalle • *n* ass
dunke • *v* knock
dur • *adj* major
dust • *n* dust, fool
dyd • *n* virtue
dyne • *n* blanket
dyp • *adj* deep, fast
dypdykke • *v* drill
dypgang • *n* draft
dypt • *adv* fast
dyr • *n* animal • *adj* expensive
dyrisk • *adj* animal
dyrke • *v* farm, grow

dytte • *v* push
dø • *v* die
døden • *n* death
dødt • *adj* flat
døgn • *n* day
døme • *n* example
dømme • *v* sentence
dør • *n* door
døsig • *adj* sleepy
døv • *adj* deaf
døy • *v* die
dåd • *n* deed
dårlig • *adj* bad, poor
dåse • *n* box

Ecuador • *n* Ecuador
edel • *adj* noble
edelstein • *n* rock, stone
editor • *n* editor
effekt • *n* effect, power
effektiv • *adj* effective
egen • *adj* proper
egenskap • *n* attribute
egentlig • *adj* proper
egna • *adj* eligible
egnet • *adj* appropriate, suitable
egoist • *n* egoist
eh • *interj* uh
eie • *v* own
eik • *n* oak
ekkel • *adj* gross, ugly
eksaminere • *v* examine
eksempel • *n* example, sample

eksemplar • *n* copy
eksistens • *n* existence
eksistere • *v* exist
ekskludere • *v* exclude
ekskrement • *n* shit
eksos • *n* exhaust
ekspandere • *v* expand
ekspeditør • *n* clerk
eksplodere • *v* explode
ekstrahere • *v* extract
ekstrakt • *n* abstract, extract
ekte • *adj* true • *v* wed
ektemann • *n* husband
ektevie • *v* wed
eldes • *v* date
elefant • *n* elephant
elektronisk • *adj* electronic
elendig • *adj* poor
elg • *n* moose
eller • *conj* nor, or
elleve • *num* eleven
elske • *v* love
elskling • *n* love
elv • *n* river
emergens • *n* emergence
enda • *det* another • *adv* still, yet
ende • *n* end
endelig • *adj* ultimate
endeløs • *adj* eternal
endre • *v* turn
energi • *n* energy
energisk • *adj* exuberant
enerverende • *v* annoying
eneste • *adj* sole
enestående • *adj* brilliant
engasjement • *n* commitment, zeal
engasjert • *adj* zealous
engelsk • *adj* English
engstelig • *adj* afraid, eerie
enhver • *pron* anyone • *det* each

enighet • *n* agreement
enkel • *adj* easy, light
enkelt • *adj* elementary
enkelte • *det* certain
enn • *conj* but • *prep* than
ennå • *adv* yet
enorm • *adj* vast
enslig • *adj* sole
ensomhet • *n* loneliness
entre • *v* board
entré • *n* entrance
entreprenør • *n* entrepreneur
eple • *n* apple
epletre • *n* apple
epost • *n* email
erfare • *v* experience
erfaring • *n* experience
ergerlig • *adj* annoyed
erigere • *v* erect
erklære • *v* pronounce
ernæring • *n* nourishment, nutrition
ert • *n* pea
erverve • *v* purchase
ervervelse • *n* purchase
esel • *n* ass
eske • *n* box
Estland • *n* Estonia
etablere • *v* establish
etappe • *n* leg
etikett • *n* label, tag
Etiopia • *n* Ethiopia
etter • *adv* after • *prep* by
etterfølgende • *adj* adjacent
etterlate • *v* leave
ettermiddag • *n* afternoon
etterpå • *adv* after
etterspørsel • *n* demand
ettertenksom • *adj* pensive
evakuering • *n* evacuation
eventyrlysten • *adj* adventurous

evidens • *n* evidence
evig • *adj* eternal
evinnelig • *adj* eternal
evne • *n* ability, head
explosjon • *n* blast

fabelaktig • *adj* fabulous
fabrikk • *n* factory, mill
fader • *n* father
fag • *n* trade
fagfelt • *n* field
fakke • *v* nail
faktisk • *adj* actual
faktor • *n* factor
faktorisere • *v* expand, factor
faktum • *n* fact
fakultet • *n* school
falk • *n* kestrel
fall • *n* fall
falle • *v* fall
familie • *n* family
fan • *n* fan
fane • *n* banner, color
fang • *n* lap
fange • *v* catch, nail
fangst • *n* take
fantasi • *n* imagination
fantastisk • *adj* fantastic
far • *n* father
fare • *n* danger • *v* go
farfar • *n* grandfather
farge • *n* color
fargeekte • *adj* fast
fargelegge • *v* color

fargerik • *adj* gay
fargetone • *n* color
farmor • *n* grandmother
farvel • *interj* bye, goodbye
fasade • *n* front
fascinasjon • *n* fascination
fascinere • *v* entrance
fascinert • *n* fascination
fast • *adj* fast, solid
faste • *v* fast
faster • *n* aunt
fastland • *n* mainland
fastlegge • *v* set
fastslå • *v* ascertain, establish
fatal • *adj* fatal
fatte • *v* comprehend, get, understand
fattig • *adj* poor
favoritt • *adj* favourite
fe • *n* cattle
feber • *n* fever
fedme • *n* obesity
feiging • *n* chicken
feil • *adj* wrong
feile • *v* fail
feilgrep • *n* mistake
feilvare • *n* second
feit • *adj* fat
felle • *n* trap
felles • *adj* mutual
felt • *n* field
fem • *num* five
femi • *adj* gay
femte • *adj* fifth
femten • *num* fifteen
femti • *num* fifty
fengsel • *n* jail, prison
fengsle • *v* imprison
fengslende • *adj* magnetic
ferdsel • *n* traffic
ferie • *n* vacation

fersk • *adj* fresh, sweet
feste • *v* fix
festlig • *adj* gay
fetter • *n* cousin
fiasko • *n* failure
fiende • *n* enemy
fiendtlig • *adj* enemy
fike • *v* slap
fikse • *v* fix
fiksere • *v* fix
filmmateriale • *n* footage
filter • *n* filter
fin • *adj* fine, nice
finanser • *n* finance
finger • *n* digit, finger
finish • *n* finish
finknuse • *v* crush
Finland • *n* Finland
finlesing • *n* scrutiny
finne • *v* find
fint • *adj* fine
fiolett • *n* purple
fire • *num* four
fis • *n* wind
fisk • *n* fish
fiske • *v* fish
fisking • *n* fishing
fix • *n* fix
fjerde • *adj* fourth
fjern • *adj* far, remote
fjerne • *v* disappear
fjernkontroll • *n* remote
fjert • *n* wind
fjes • *n* face
fjollete • *adj* silly
fjorten • *num* fourteen
fjøs • *n* stable
flagg • *n* banner, flag
flaks • *n* fortune
flamingo • *n* flamingo
flamme • *n* light

flaske • *n* bottle
flat • *adj* flat
flate • *n* face
flau • *adj* embarrassed
flekk • *n* dirt, mark, spot
fleksibel • *adj* flexible
flink • *adj* good, proficient
flipp • *n* toss
flippe • *v* toss
flittig • *adj* diligent, zealous
flo • *n* flow
flod • *n* river
floke • *n* complexity
flokk • *n* crowd, pride
flom • *n* flow
flomme • *v* flow
flott • *adj* fine
fly • *v* fly • *n* plane
flyselskap • *n* airline
flytende • *adj* liquid
flytte • *v* move
fløda • *v* flow
fløte • *n* cream
fløyma • *v* flow
flå • *v* speed
flått • *n* tick
folie • *n* leaf
folk • *n* folk, people
folkehav • *n* crowd
folkemengde • *n* crowd
folkemord • *n* genocide
folkestyre • *n* democracy
for • *prep* by, for • *adv* too
fora • *n* forum
forarget • *adj* annoyed
forbannet • *adj* annoyed
forbedre • *v* better, improve
forbehold • *n* reservation
forbeholde • *v* reserve
forbi • *prep* past
forbindelse • *n* connection

forbli • *v* stay
forbløffende • *adj* amazing
forbrenne • *v* burn
forbruk • *n* expenditure
forbruke • *v* consume
forbudt • *det* no
forby • *v* ban, forbid
forderve • *v* spoil
fordi • *conj* for, since
fordom • *n* bias, prejudice
fordomsfri • *adj* candid
fordomsfull • *adj* prejudiced
fordreie • *v* distort
fordunkle • *v* cloud
foredrag • *n* talk
foregå • *v* happen
foregående • *adj* adjacent
foreldet • *adj* dated, legacy
forelesning • *n* talk
forenkles • *v* simplify
foreslå • *v* offer, propose
foretagende • *n* enterprise
forfatter • *n* writer
forferdelig • *adj* awful • *adv* terrible
forfremme • *v* up
forfølge • *v* chase, tail
forfølgelse • *n* chase
forfølger • *n* tail
forførisk • *adj* magnetic
forgude • *v* god
forhandle • *v* negotiate
forhandling • *n* negotiation
forhekset • *n* fascination
forheksing • *n* fascination
forhindre • *v* deter
forhindring • *n* wall
forhold • *n* ratio, relationship
forhåpning • *n* trust
forkaste • *v* abolish
forkastning • *n* fault

forklaring • *n* account
forlange • *v* demand
forlate • *v* abandon, forgive, forsake, leave, part
Forlokkende • *adj* intriguing
forløp • *n* march
formannskap • *n* presidency
formasjon • *n* formation
formel • *n* spell
formell • *adj* formal
formidle • *v* convey
forminske • *v* contract, decrease
forminskning • *n* contraction
formode • *v* suppose
formue • *n* substance
formørke • *v* cloud
formål • *n* end, goal
formålstjenlig • *adj* appropriate
fornektelse • *n* denial
fornuft • *n* reason
fornuftig • *adj* reasonable
fornye • *v* innovate
fornøyd • *adj* content, satisfied
fornøyelse • *n* pleasure
forpleining • *n* keep
forpult • *adj* fucking
forresten • *phr* by the way
forretning • *n* business, shop
forretningsområde • *n* industry
forringe • *v* decrease
forringelse • *n* decrease
forråd • *n* reserve, store
forsamling • *n* assembly
forsegling • *n* seal
forsikre • *v* warrant
forsiktig • *adj* soft, vigilant
forsinkelse • *n* delay
forsinket • *adj* belated
forskjell • *n* distinction
forskjellig • *adj* different

F

forskjønne • *v* beautify
forskudd • *n* advance
forslag • *n* offer, suggestion
forsone • *v* reconcile
forstand • *n* mind, wit
forsterkning • *n* gain, power
forstyrre • *v* bother, disturb
forstørre • *v* magnify
forstå • *v* appreciate, comprehend, get, know, read, see, understand
forsvar • *n* defense
forsvare • *v* defend
forsvinne • *v* go
forsvinning • *n* disappearance
forsøk • *n* attempt
forsøke • *v* attempt, try
forsøkskanin • *n* guinea pig
fort • *adv* quickly
fortelle • *v* tell
fortid • *n* past
fortie • *v* conceal
fortrinnsvis • *adv* rather
fortrylle • *v* entrance
fortryllet • *n* fascination
fortrylling • *n* fascination
fortsette • *v* keep
fortvile • *v* despair
fortære • *v* consume
forum • *n* forum
forunderlig • *adj* puzzling
foruten • *conj* but
forutgående • *adj* adjacent
forutsetning • *n* condition
forutsette • *v* suppose
forutsi • *v* forecast
forvandle • *v* turn
forveksle • *v* confuse
forverre • *v* deteriorate, suffer
forverres • *v* deteriorate
forvikling • *n* complexity

forvirre • *v* confuse
forvise • *v* abandon, exile
forvisning • *n* ban
forvrenge • *v* distort
forward • *n* forward
foræde • *v* burn
forårsake • *v* effect
fotball • *n* football, soccer
fotografere • *v* photograph, picture
fotografi • *n* photography
Fr • *n* Mrs
fra • *prep* from
frakk • *n* coat
frakt • *n* cargo
frambringelse • *n* product
frame • *n* frame
framkalle • *v* evoke
framover • *adv* forward
framtid • *n* future
framtidig • *adj* forward
frank • *adj* frank
Frankrike • *n* France
franskmenn • *n* French
frastøtende • *adj* ugly
fratrukket • *prep* less
fredag • *n* Friday
frekk • *adj* naughty, saucy
frekvens • *n* frequency
fremmedgjøre • *v* alienate
fremragende • *adj* outstanding
fremre • *adj* forward
fri • *adj* clear, free • *v* propose
fridom • *n* freedom
frie • *n* base
frigi • *v* free
frigjøre • *v* free, liberate
frisk • *adj* sound
friste • *v* tempt
front • *n* front
frosk • *n* frog**

fru • *n* Mrs
frustrasjon • *n* despair
fryktelig • *adv* terrible
fryse • *v* freeze, ice
frøken • *n* miss
fuktig • *adj* wet
full • *adj* full
fullføre • *v* finish
fullstendig • *adv* entirely • *adj* full
fundament • *n* foundation
fundamental • *n* fundamental
fundere • *v* think
fungere • *v* work
funksjon • *n* function
funn • *n* find
fuske • *v* cheat
fylle • *v* stuff
fyllestgjørende • *det* enough
fyllesyke • *n* hangover
fyr • *n* fire
fyre • *v* fire
fyrstikk • *n* match
fyrverkeri • *n* firework
fysisk • *adj* physical
færre • *det* fewer • *adj* less
føde • *n* food
fødselsdag • *n* birthday
fødselshjelper • *n* midwife
født • *adj* born
føflekk • *n* mole
føle • *v* feel
følelse • *n* touch
følge • *v* follow
følgende • *adj* adjacent, next
følsom • *adj* feeling, sensitive
før • *adv* before • *adj* fast
føre • *v* bear, lead, transport
fører • *n* leader
første • *adj* head
førstis • *n* freshman

førti • *num* forty
få • *det* few • *v* get, may, receive, retain
får • *n* sheep

Gabon • *n* Gabon
gal • *adj* bad, crazy, mad, wrong
galakse • *n* galaxy
gale • *v* crow
galen • *adj* crazy
galning • *n* crazy, nut
galt • *adj* wrong
Gambia • *n* Gambia
gammel • *adj* old
gang • *n* march, time
ganske • *adv* quite, rather
garantere • *v* guarantee, warrant
garanti • *n* guarantee
garantist • *n* guarantee
gardere • *v* protect
geipe • *v* poke
gelender • *n* rail
generell • *adj* general
generisk • *adj* generic
genial • *adj* brilliant
Georgia • *n* Georgia
gevinst • *n* take
Ghana • *n* Ghana
gi • *v* give, hand
gidde • *v* bother
gift • *adj* married • *n* poison
giftig • *adj* poisonous
gips • *n* cast

girspak • *n* stick
gisp • *n* gasp
gispe • *v* gasp
gissa • *v* guess
gissel • *n* hostage
gjedde • *n* pike
gjeld • *n* debt
gjelde • *v* fix
gjeldende • *adj* current
gjemme • *v* conceal
gjeng • *n* bunch
gjennom • *prep* through
gjennomføre • *v* pull
gjennomsiktig • *adj* clear, transparent
gjennomskuelig • *adj* transparent
gjennomsynlig • *adj* transparent
gjensidig • *adj* mutual
gjenstand • *n* object
gjerdesmett • *n* wren
gjerning • *n* deed
gjerrig • *adj* stingy
gjestfri • *adj* hospitable
gjetning • *n* guess
gjette • *v* guess
gjær • *n* yeast
gjørme • *n* mud
glad • *adj* bright, gay, happy
glede • *n* happiness
gli • *v* slide, slip
glidelås • *n* fly
glitre • *adj* sparkling
glorie • *n* glory
gnist • *n* spark
god • *adj* good
godkjenne • *v* sanction
godkjennelse • *n* sanction
godt • *adj* good
godta • *v* accept

godteri • *n* candy
grad • *n* degree
grafisk • *adj* graphic
granske • *v* scrutinize
gratis • *adv* free
grave • *v* dig
grei • *adj* cool, sound
greie • *n* thing
grein • *n* branch
Grekenland • *n* Greece
gren • *n* branch
grenseland • *n* march
gresk • *adj* Greek
gress • *n* herb
gresshoppe • *n* grasshopper
gretten • *adj* churlish, grumpy
gribb • *n* vulture
gripe • *v* seize, take
gris • *n* pig
grotesk • *adj* grotesque
grov • *adj* rude
gru • *n* horror
grundig • *adj* comprehensive, thorough
grunn • *n* cause
grunnlegge • *v* found
grunnlov • *n* constitution
grunnmur • *n* foundation
grusom • *adj* awful, cruel, gruesome
grusomhet • *n* atrocity
grønn • *adj* green
grå • *adj* gray
grålysning • *n* dawn
gråte • *v* water
gud • *n* god
Gud • *n* God
Gudskjelov • *interj* for God's sake
gul • *adj* yellow
gulrot • *n* carrot

gulv • *n* floor
gummi • *n* condom, rubber
gylf • *n* fly
gyllen • *adj* golden
gymnastikk • *n* gymnastics
gynge • *v* rock
gæren • *adj* crazy
gærning • *n* crazy, nut
gøyme • *v* conceal
gå • *v* go, run, walk, work
gård • *n* yard

ha • *v* have
hadet • *interj* goodbye
hage • *n* garden
hagl • *n* hail, shot
hagle • *v* hail
Haiti • *n* Haiti
hake • *n* chin
hakke • *n* pick
hakkespett • *n* woodpecker
hale • *n* tail
halla • *interj* hello
hallo • *interj* hello
hals • *n* neck, throat
ham • *n* skin
hamp • *n* cannabis
han • *det* he
handel • *n* trade
handhilse • *v* shake
handle • *v* move, shop
handling • *n* shopping
handskrift • *n* hand
hane • *n* rooster

hans • *det* his
hanske • *n* glove
hard • *adj* hard
hardne • *v* cool
harmoni • *n* harmony
hasj • *n* weed
hastighet • *n* speed
hat • *n* hatred
hate • *v* hate
hatt • *n* hat
haug • *n* crowd, pile
hauk • *n* kestrel
haus • *n* skull
have • *n* garden
havne • *v* end up
hei • *interj* goodbye, hello
heiarop • *n* cheer
heie • *v* cheer
heim • *n* home
heis • *n* elevator
heisann • *interj* hello
heit • *adj* hot
hel • *adj* full, whole
heldig • *adj* happy, lucky
hele • *det* all • *v* heal
heler • *n* receiver
helhet • *n* whole
hell • *n* happiness
Hellas • *n* Greece
hellenesk • *n* Greek
heller • *adv* rather
hellig • *adj* sacred
helling • *n* slope
helse • *n* constitution
helt • *n* hero • *adv* quite, whole
heltids • *adj* full-time
helvete • *n* hell
hemmelig • *adj* secret
henge • *v* suspend
henne • *det* her
hennes • *det* her

hensikt • *n* mind
hensiktsmessig • *adj* appropriate
hensynsløs • *adj* ruthless
hente • *v* fetch
her • *adv* here
herav • *adv* hence
heretter • *adv* forward
hermetikkboks • *n* can
heroin • *n* heroin
herr • *n* Mr.
herre • *n* master
Herre • *n* God
herrer • *n* gentleman
herretoalett • *n* gentleman
hest • *n* horse
het • *adj* hot
heterofil • *adj* straight
hetetokt • *n* heat
hett • *adj* hot
heve • *v* lift
hevn • *n* revenge
hilsen • *n* greeting
himmel • *n* heaven, sky
hinte • *v* hint
historie • *n* history, story, tale
hit • *adv* here • *adj* hit
hive • *v* throw
hjelm • *n* helmet
hjelp • *interj* help
hjelpe • *v* help
hjelpsom • *adj* helpful, sweet
hjem • *n* home, pad
hjemland • *n* home
hjemlig • *adj* domestic
hjemme • *n* home
hjemmelekse • *n* homework
hjerne • *n* brain
hjort • *n* deer
hockeykølle • *n* stick
hode • *n* head

hodekål • *n* cabbage
hoff • *n* court
hol • *n* hole
holde • *v* do, hold, store
Holland • *n* Netherlands
homo • *adj* gay
homoseksuell • *adj* gay
homse • *adj* gay
homsete • *adj* gay
Honduras • *n* Honduras
honningbie • *n* honey bee
hopp • *n* jump • *v* leap
hoppe • *v* jump, leap
hor • *n* adultery
horekunde • *n* trick
horisont • *n* horizon
hos • *prep* next to
hovedkvarter • *n* base
hovmodig • *adj* supercilious
hud • *n* skin
hudfarge • *n* color
huke • *v* hook
hukommelse • *n* mind
hulepinnsvin • *n* porcupine
hull • *n* hole
hummer • *n* lobster
humør • *n* humour, mood
hun • *pron* she
hund • *n* dog
hundre • *num* hundred
hungre • *v* hunger
hunkjønn • *adj* feminine
hurtig • *adv* fast • *adj* rapid
hus • *n* house
husbond • *n* husband
husdyr • *adj* domestic
hushjelp • *n* help
huske • *v* mind
huslig • *adj* domestic
husvarm • *phr* at home
hva • *interj* huh • *pron* what

hvem • *pron* who
hvems • *det* whose
hver • *det* every
hvese • *n* hiss
hvetebrødsdager • *n* honeymoon
hvin • *n* whine
hvine • *v* whine
hvis • *conj* if • *det* whose
Hviterussland • *n* Belarus
hvitvasking • *n* money laundering
hvor • *conj* where
hvordan • *adv* how
hvorfor • *interj* why
hvorved • *adv* whereby
hyene • *n* hyena
hyggelig • *adj* nice
hyl • *n* whine
hyle • *v* howl, scream, whine
hylster • *n* case
hypothek • *n* mortgage
hyppig • *adj* frequent • *adv* often
hyppighet • *n* rate
hytte • *n* cabin
høflig • *adj* polite
høre • *v* hear, listen, read
høring • *n* hearing
høste • *v* harvest
høsting • *n* harvest
høvel • *n* plane
høvelig • *adj* proper
høvisk • *adj* proper
høvle • *v* plane
høy • *adj* high
høyere • *adv* above
høyne • *v* up
høyst • *adv* most
håndskrift • *n* hand
håndtere • *v* manage

håndverk • *n* trade
håpe • *v* hope

i • *prep* in
idag • *adv* today
idé • *n* idea
identifisere • *v* spot
idet • *conj* as
idiot • *n* ass, idiot
idolisere • *v* god
ignorere • *v* ignore
iherdig • *adj* diligent
illustrasjon • *n* illustration
imens • *adv* meanwhile
imidlertid • *adv* however
imot • *prep* against
imperium • *n* empire
implisere • *v* imply
imponere • *v* impress
imponerende • *adj* impressive
impressario • *n* manager
imøtekommende • *adj* forthcoming
indeks • *n* index
India • *n* India
indikator • *n* indicator
industriell • *adj* industrial
infeksjon • *n* infection
inflasjon • *n* inflation
influere • *v* affect
informasjon • *n* information
informere • *v* inform
ingen • *det* no • *pron* no one

ingenting • *pron* nothing • *n* nothingness
initiativ • *n* initiative
inn • *adv* in
innbilning • *n* imagination
inndragning • *n* seizure
inne • *adv* in, inside
inneha • *v* possess
innen • *prep* by, within
innenfor • *prep* within
innesluttet • *adj* evasive
innflyging • *n* approach
innflytelse • *n* power
inngang • *n* entrance
inngi • *v* file
innhegne • *v* pen
innhegning • *n* pen
innhold • *n* index
innholdsfortegnelse • *n* index
innkjøring • *n* approach
innlede • *v* open
innlysende • *adj* obvious
innprente • *v* brand
innramme • *v* frame
innringing • *n* bell
innrømme • *v* grant
innrømmelse • *n* grant
innskrenket • *adj* narrow-minded
innstilling • *n* mind
inntekt • *n* income
inntil • *prep* till
inntreffe • *v* happen, occur
innvending • *n* complaint, objection
innvilge • *v* grant
insinuere • *v* imply
insolvent • *v* bankrupt
installatør • *n* installer
integral • *n* integral
intellekt • *n* mind, wit

intelligent • *adj* clever, intelligent
intensjon • *n* mind
interaksjon • *n* interaction
interesse • *n* stake
interessert • *adj* interested
interferens • *n* interference
Internett • *n* Internet
intervall • *n* interval
intervensjon • *n* intervention
intervju • *n* interview
introduksjon • *n* introduction
introdusert • *v* set
investere • *v* invest
Iran • *n* Iran
Irland • *n* Ireland
irritende • *adj* irritating
irritere • *v* bother, irritate
irriterende • *v* annoying • *adj* irritating
irritert • *adj* annoyed
is • *n* ice
isbelagt • *adj* icy
isbit • *n* rock
ise • *v* ice
isete • *adj* icy
islagt • *adj* icy
islegge • *v* ice
isnende • *adj* icy
isolere • *v* isolate
isse • *n* crown
isteden • *adv* instead
iver • *n* zeal
iverksetting • *n* implementation
ivrig • *adj* eager, zealous

ja • *part* yeah, yes
jakt • *n* chase, hunt
jakte • *v* hunt
jamre • *v* whine
jatte • *v* agree
jeans • *n* jeans
jeg • *pron* me
jevn • *adj* even
jevnbyrdig • *n* match
jo • *part* yes
jobb • *n* job, work
jobbe • *v* work
jokke • *v* fuck
jol • *n* Christmas
jord • *n* dirt, earth
jordbruk • *n* agriculture
jordfestelse • *n* funeral
jordnøtt • *n* peanut
jordsmonn • *n* soil
journalist • *n* journalist
journalistikk • *n* journalism
jubileum • *n* anniversary
juice • *n* juice
jukse • *v* cheat
juksepave • *n* cheat
jul • *n* Christmas
jungel • *n* jungle
jus • *n* juice
justere • *v* adjust, set
jævla • *adj* bloody, fucking
jødisk • *adj* Jewish

kabal • *n* patience
kabin • *n* cabin

Kabinett • *n* ministry
kald • *adj* cold, cool
kaldt • *adj* cold
kalle • *v* call, name
kalosj • *n* rubber
Kambodsja • *n* Cambodia
kamerat • *n* boy
kammer • *n* chamber
kamp • *n* fight, leg, match
kampestein • *n* rock
kan • *v* may
kanal • *n* channel
kanarifugl • *n* canary
kanarigul • *n* canary
kandidat • *n* candidate
kandissukker • *n* rock
kanin • *n* rabbit
kanonisere • *v* saint
kanskje • *adv* maybe, perhaps
kant • *n* border, edge, side
kaos • *n* chaos
kapital • *n* capital
kapring • *n* piracy
karakter • *n* character, mark
karakteristisk • *adj* characteristic
karbon • *n* carbon
kasse • *n* box, chest
kast • *n* throw, toss
kaste • *v* cast, throw, throw away, toss
katte • *v* cat
kausjonere • *v* guarantee
kavallerist • *n* horse
keeper • *n* keeper
keyboard • *n* keyboard
kidnappe • *v* kidnap
killing • *n* kid
Kina • *n* China
kinesisk • *n* Chinese
kino • *n* picture

J
K

Kirgisistan • *n* Kyrgyzstan
Kiribati • *n* Kiribati
kirurg • *n* surgeon
kirurgi • *n* surgery
kiste • *n* case, chest
kjapp • *adj* fast
kjapt • *adv* fast
kje • *n* kid
kjed • *adj* bored
kjede • *n* chain
kjedelig • *adj* dull
kjeft • *n* face, mouth
kjekk • *adj* handsome
kjeks • *n* biscuit
kjemi • *n* chemistry
kjempe • *v* fight, struggle
kjempepanda • *n* panda
kjempeviktig • *adj* vital
kjendis • *n* star
kjenne • *v* feel, know
kjepp • *n* stick
kjetting • *n* chain
kjeve • *n* jaw
kjole • *n* dress
kjæle • *v* pet
kjær • *adj* dear
kjære • *adj* dear • *n* love, sugar
kjæreste • *n* love
kjærtegne • *v* pct
kjøleskap • *n* refrigerator
kjølne • *v* chill
kjønn • *n* gender, sex
kjønnslig • *adj* sexy
kjøp • *n* purchase
kjøpe • *v* buy, purchase
kladd • *n* draft
kladde • *v* draft
klage • *n* complaint
klar • *adj* brilliant, clear, ready, up
klare • *v* handle, manage

klase • *n* bunch, cluster
klasse • *n* class
klasserom • *n* classroom
klaviatur • *n* keyboard
kle • *v* become, dress
klem • *n* hug
klemme • *v* hug, squeeze
klenge • *v* cling
klesvask • *n* laundry
klinke • *n* handle
klinkekule • *n* marble
klipp • *n* shear
klippe • *v* mow, shear • *n* rock
klok • *adj* clever
klokke • *n* watch
kloss • *n* block
klubbe • *n* club
klumsete • *adj* awkward
kluss • *n* bother
klær • *n* dress
klønete • *adj* awkward
kløver • *n* club
kløyve • *v* cleave
knapp • *n* button
knappenål • *n* pin
kne • *n* knee
knele • *v* kneel
knep • *n* trick
kneppe • *v* button
knipe • *n* fix
knipse • *v* roll
knivblad • *n* knife
knull • *n* fuck, fucking
knulle • *v* bone, fuck
knuse • *v* crush, powder, squeeze
knusende • *adj* crushing
knyttneve • *n* fist
kokaburra • *n* kookaburra
kokain • *n* cocaine
koke • *v* boil

kolhydrat • *n* carbohydrate
koloritt • *n* color
komma • *n* point
komme • *v* come
kommentere • *v* comment
kommode • *n* chest
kommunal • *adj* municipal
kompakt • *adj* solid
komparabel • *adj* comparable
komparativ • *adj* comparative
kompensere • *v* compensate
kompis • *n* boy
komplett • *adv* entirely • *adj* full
komplisert • *adj* complicated
kondisjonalis • *n* conditional
kondom • *n* condom, rubber
konfekt • *n* chocolate
konfigurere • *v* configure
konfrontere • *v* face
kongedømme • *n* kingdom
kongerike • *n* kingdom
kongeriket • *n* kingdom
kongruens • *n* agreement
konjunksjon • *n* conjunction
konkret • *adj* concrete
konkurranse • *n* competition, contest
konkurs • *v* bankrupt
konsentrasjon • *n* mind
konsern • *n* concern
konsis • *adj* succinct
konsistens • *n* consistency
konspirasjon • *n* conspiracy
konstant • *adv* always
konstitusjon • *n* constitution
konstruere • *n* building
kontakt • *n* touch
kontakte • *v* contact
kontanter • *n* cash, money
kontinent • *adj* continent
konto • *n* account

kontor • *n* office
kontorist • *n* clerk
kontraksjon • *n* contraction
kontrakt • *n* contract
kontroll • *n* check
kontrollere • *v* check, control
kopiere • *v* copy
kopp • *n* cup
kor • *n* choir
korn • *n* corn, grain
korps • *n* band
korpulent • *adj* fat, obese
korpus • *n* corpus
korrekt • *adj* proper
korridor • *n* corridor
korrigere • *v* adjust
kors • *n* cross
kort • *n* card
Kosovo • *n* Kosovo
kostbar • *adj* expensive
kraft • *n* force, power
kraftig • *adj* solid
krampe • *n* seizure
kran • *n* tap
krangel • *n* contention, quarrel, word
krangle • *v* quarrel
krasje • *n* crash
krav • *n* demand, must, requirement
kravle • *v* worm
kreativ • *adj* creative
kreditere • *v* credit
kreditt • *n* credit
kredittverdighet • *n* trust
krem • *n* cream
kremfarge • *n* cream
kretskort • *n* trace
kretsløp • *n* circuit
kreve • *v* demand
krig • *n* war

K

krigersk • *adj* belligerent
kriminalitet • *n* crime
kringkaste • *v* broadcast
kringkasting • *n* broadcast
kristendom • *n* Christianity
Kristian • *n* Christian
kriterium • *n* criterion
kritisere • *v* criticize
kroke • *v* hook
krone • *n* crown
kropp • *n* field
kroppsholdning • *n* stance
krukke • *n* jar
krydre • *v* season
krympe • *v* shrink
krype • *v* crawl, worm
kryss • *n* cross
krysse • *v* cross
kryssjekke • *v* check
krøtter • *n* cattle
kråke • *n* crow
ku • *n* cow, cue
kue • *v* cow
kuk • *n* tool
kul • *adj* cool
kulde • *n* cold
kule • *n* bullet
kull • *n* carbon, class
kulldioksid • *n* carbon
kullhydrat • *n* carbohydrate
kullsyre • *n* carbon
kultur • *n* culture
kulturgjenstand • *n* artifact
kulør • *n* color
kun • *adv* alone
kung • *n* oregano
kunne • *v* can, know, understand
kunskap • *n* science
kunst • *n* art
kunstgummi • *n* rubber

kupere • *v* dock
kupp • *n* steal
kurere • *v* heal
kurs • *n* class, course
kurv • *n* basket
kusine • *n* cousin
kutt • *n* cut
kvalitet • *n* quality
kvalm • *adj* ill
kvarter • *n* quarter
kve • *n* pen
kveg • *n* cattle
kverne • *v* grind
kveste • *v* squeeze
kvikk • *adj* quick
kvinne • *n* female
kvise • *n* spot
kvist • *n* stick
Kviterussland • *n* Belarus
kvittering • *n* receipt
kylling • *n* chicken
kyss • *n* kiss
kysse • *v* kiss
kyst • *n* coast
kødde • *v* joke, kid
kølle • *n* club
kål • *n* cabbage

la • *v* let
ladd • *n* lad
ladning • *n* charge
lag • *n* side
lage • *v* make, put out
lager • *n* store, storage**

lagre • *v* file, save, store
lakk • *n* paint
lakkere • *v* paint
laks • *n* salmon
laksfisk • *n* salmon
lam • *n* lamb
lamme • *v* stun
lampe • *n* lamp
lamslå • *v* stun
land • *n* land
landbruk • *n* agriculture
lande • *v* land
landhandel • *n* grocery
landsby • *n* village
landsens • *adj* country
landskap • *n* scenery
lang • *adj* long
langsom • *adj* slow
langsomme • *adj* slow
langsomt • *adj* slow • *adv* slowly
langt • *adv* far
Laos • *n* Laos
larve • *n* caterpillar
laser • *n* laser
laste • *v* load
latskap • *n* sloth
latter • *n* laugh, laughter
laurbær • *n* bay
laurbærblad • *n* bay
lav • *adj* low
le • *v* laugh
lede • *v* manage, master
ledelse • *n* direction
leder • *n* head, leader
ledig • *adj* agile, free
lediggang • *n* sloth
ledsager • *n* date
legg • *n* calf
legge • *v* lay
legislativ • *adj* legislative

lei • *adj* sorry
leie • *n* lie
leieboer • *n* tenant
leire • *n* mud
leite • *v* look
lek • *n* game
leke • *v* play
lekkasje • *n* leak
lekke • *v* leak
lekker • *adj* hot
lekse • *n* homework
lem • *n* member
lengte • *v* long
lenke • *n* chain
leppe • *n* lip
lesbe • *adj* lesbian
lese • *v* read
lesere • *n* audience
Lesotho • *n* Lesotho
lete • *v* search
lett • *adj* easy, light
leve • *v* live
levende • *adj* alive, vital
levere • *v* deliver
levetid • *n* life
Liberia • *n* Liberia
Libya • *n* Libya
lide • *v* suffer
ligg • *n* fuck
ligge • *v* go, lie
lik • *adj* equal • *prep* like
like • *adv* as • *v* like, love • *n* match
likemann • *n* match
likevel • *adv* still
likne • *v* resemble
likning • *n* equation
likt • *adv* evenly
liktorn • *n* corn
likvid • *adj* liquid
lilla • *n* purple**

lillesøster • *n* sister
lim • *n* glue
lineær • *adj* linear
linje • *n* line
linse • *n* lens
Lisboa • *n* Lisbon
Lissabon • *n* Lisbon
Litauen • *n* Lithuania
liten • *adj* little, small
liv • *n* life
live • *adv* live
livlig • *adj* bright, gay
livsoppholdende • *adj* vital
livsstil • *n* lifestyle
livstid • *n* life
livsviktig • *adj* vital
ljuge • *v* lie
loddtrekning • *n* draw
logikk • *n* logic
logisk • *adj* logical
logistikk • *n* logistics
lojalitet • *n* loyalty
lokal • *adj* local
lokalisere • *v* localize
lokalisering • *n* localization
lokk • *n* lid
lokkende • *adj* magnetic
lommepenger • *n* spend
loppe • *v* lift, pluck
lort • *n* shit
losjere • *v* board
losse • *v* discharge, light
lov • *n* law
love • *v* promise
loven • *n* law
lovnad • *n* word
lue • *n* hat
luftballong • *n* balloon
luftskip • *n* balloon
lugg • *n* bang
lukke • *v* close

lukket • *adj* closed, evasive
lukte • *v* smell
lure • *v* cheat, fool, kid, trick
Luxembourg • *n* Luxembourg
Luxemburg • *n* Luxembourg
ly • *n* shelter
lyd • *n* people, sound
lydighet • *n* obedience
lykke • *n* happiness
lykkelig • *adj* happy
lyktestolpe • *n* lamppost
lyn • *n* lightning
lynglimt • *n* lightning
lys • *n* blond, candle, light • *adj* bright
lyse • *v* shine
lysende • *adj* brilliant
lyst • *adj* light
lystig • *adj* bright
lystre • *v* listen
lytte • *v* listen
lyve • *v* lie
lære • *v* learn, study, teach
løft • *n* lift
løfte • *v* lift • *n* promise
løgn • *n* lie
løk • *n* onion
løpe • *v* chase, run
Løpe • *n* run
løper • *n* bishop
løpetid • *n* season
løs • *adj* free
løslate • *v* free
løsning • *n* answer
løssluppenhet • *n* abandon
løv • *n* leaf
løve • *n* lion
løyve • *n* leave
lågtrykksområde • *n* low
lån • *n* loan
låne • *v* lend, spot**

lår • *n* thigh
lått • *n* laugh
låve • *n* barn

maddik • *n* maggot
Madrid • *n* Madrid
magasin • *n* magazine
mage • *n* stomach
mager • *adj* lean
magisk • *adj* magic
magnet • *n* magnet
magnetisk • *adj* magnetic
majoritet • *n* majority
Makedonia • *n* Macedonia
makk • *n* worm
makt • *n* power
maktesløs • *adj* powerless
maktutøvelse • *n* reign
Malawi • *n* Malawi
male • *v* color, grind, paint, purr
maleri • *n* painting
maling • *n* paint
malplassert • *adj* inappropriate
manager • *n* manager
mandag • *n* Monday
manet • *n* jellyfish
mangel • *n* lack, want
mangle • *v* lack
manifest • *adj* manifest
manifestere • *v* manifest
mannlig • *adj* male
manuskript • *n* manuscript
mappe • *n* folder
mareritt • *n* nightmare

mark • *n* worm
marked • *n* market
markedsplass • *n* market
markere • *v* highlight
marmor • *n* marble
Mars • *n* Mars
marsj • *n* march
marsjere • *v* march
maskinvare • *n* hardware
massakre • *n* massacre
massakrere • *v* massacre
masse • *n* substance
massiv • *adj* solid
masterkopi • *n* master
mat • *n* food
match • *n* match
mate • *v* feed
matematikk • *n* mathematics
materiale • *n* material, stuff
materiell • *adj* material
mating • *n* feed
matlyst • *n* appetite
matolje • *n* oil
matros • *n* sailor
matt • *adj* dull
matvarer • *n* shopping
med • *prep* by • *adj* game, up
meddele • *v* notify
medføre • *v* imply
medisin • *n* medicine
meg • *pron* me
meget • *adv* most
meieriprodukter • *n* dairy
mekaniker • *n* mechanic
mektig • *adj* mighty
melankoli • *n* sadness
melkebutikk • *n* dairy
melkeprodukter • *n* dairy
mellom • *prep* among, between
mellomnavn • *n* middle name
melodi • *n* melody

L
M

men • *conj* but • *adv* however
mene • *v* think
mengde • *n* crowd
menighet • *n* ward
mening • *n* meaning, opinion
menneske • *n* man
menneskeaktig • *adj* human
menneskelig • *adj* human
mens • *conj* as
meny • *n* menu
merke • *n* accent, mark • *v* label
merkelapp • *n* tag
merkelig • *adj* funny, strange
Merkur • *n* Mercury
mester • *n* master
mesterstykke • *n* masterpiece
mesterverk • *n* masterpiece
mestre • *v* master
metal • *n* metal
meteoritt • *n* meteorite
meteorolog • *n* meteorologist
metropolitt • *adj* metropolitan
mett • *adj* full, satisfied
Mexico • *n* Mexico
midje • *n* waist
midt • *n* center
midterst • *adj* middle
midtpunkt • *n* center
Mikronesiaføderasjonen • *n* Micronesia
mikse • *v* mix
militær • *adj* military
milliard • *n* billion
million • *num* million
min • *pron* me, mine • *det* my
mindre • *adj* less
mindreårig • *n* infant
mine • *n* expression, face, mine
minelegge • *v* mine
mineral • *n* mineral
mineralvann • *n* mineral

minne • *n* mind
minus • *prep* less
minutt • *n* minute
misbruk • *n* abuse
misbruke • *v* abuse
misforstå • *v* mistake
mishandle • *v* abuse
misjon • *n* mission
misjonær • *n* missionary
mislike • *v* dislike
missil • *n* missile
mistanke • *n* suspicion
miste • *v* lose
misunnelig • *adj* envious, jealous
misære • *n* failure
mjøl • *n* flour
mobil • *adj* mobile
moden • *adj* mature
moderne • *adj* modern
modig • *adj* bold, brave
modnes • *v* season
Moldova • *n* Moldova
molekyl • *n* molecule
moment • *n* moment
Monaco • *n* Monaco
Mongolia • *n* Mongolia
monoton • *adj* flat
monster • *n* monster
montere • *v* mount
morbid • *adj* morbid
mord • *n* murder
morder • *n* killer
morfar • *n* grandfather
mormor • *n* grandmother
moro • *n* fun
morsom • *adj* gay
mosjonere • *v* train
moster • *n* aunt
mot • *prep* against, for, toward
mote • *n* fashion, mode

motkraft • *n* resistance
motorsykkel • *n* bike
motorveg • *n* highway
motorvei • *n* highway
motsatt • *adj* adjacent, opposite
motsigende • *adj* contradictory
motstand • *n* resistance
motstå • *v* resist, stand
motstående • *adj* adverse
motta • *v* accept, copy, get, retain
mottak • *n* take
mottaker • *n* receiver
muggen • *adj* sullen
muligens • *adv* perhaps
mulighet • *n* chance, possibility
multiplisere • *v* yield
munk • *n* monk
munn • *n* mouth
munnfull • *n* bite, mouthful
munnharmonika • *n* harmonica
munnspill • *n* harmonica
murmeldyr • *n* marmot
mus • *n* mouse
museum • *n* museum
musikk • *n* music
muskel • *n* muscle
must • *n* must
mutter • *n* nut
Myanmar • *n* Myanmar
mye • *det* much
myk • *adj* soft
myndig • *phr* of age • *adj* major
myndighetsalder • *n* majority
mynt • *n* coin
myntkast • *n* toss
myrde • *v* murder
mysterium • *n* mystery
mystiskt • *adj* mysterious
møkk • *n* shit

møkkete • *adj* filthy
mølle • *n* mill
møne • *n* ridge
mørk • *adj* black, dark
mørke • *n* dark, night
må • *v* have to, may
mål • *n* end, goal, measure, purpose
måleapparat • *n* instrument
måler • *n* indicator
måling • *n* measurement
målsetting • *n* goal
måne • *n* moon
måned • *n* month
månen • *n* moon
måte • *n* way
måtte • *v* must

nabo • *n* neighbour
naboer • *n* neighborhood
naboskap • *n* neighborhood
naken • *adj* naked
narkotika • *n* substance
narr • *n* fool
narre • *v* fool, trick
nasjon • *n* nation
NATO • *n* NATO
natt • *n* night
nattbord • *n* nightstand
nattesøvn • *n* night
nattklubb • *n* club
natur • *n* nature
navigere • *v* navigate
navn • *n* name

navngi • *v* name
nebb • *n* bill
ned • *adv* down
nedbrytende • *adj* disruptive
nedbrytes • *v* deteriorate
nede • *adv* down
nederlag • *n* defeat
Nederland • *n* Netherlands
nederlandsk • *adj* Netherlands
nedgang • *n* decline, fall
nedlaste • *v* download
nedlastning • *n* download
nedlatende • *adj*
  condescending
nedoverbakke • *n* slope
nedskrive • *v* book
negasjon • *n* denial
negativ • *adj* negative
nei • *n* no
nekting • *n* denial
nemning • *n* designation
nennsomhet • *n* care
Neptun • *n* Neptune
neste • *adj* adjacent, next
nestemann • *n* next
nesten • *adv* about
nett • *n* net, network
nettbrett • *n* tablet computer
nettopp • *adj* just
nettverk • *n* network
neve • *n* fist
nevne • *v* name
ni • *num* nine
nidkjær • *adj* zealous
nifs • *adj* eerie
Nigeria • *n* Nigeria
nikk • *n* nod
nikke • *v* nod
nitten • *num* nineteen
nitti • *num* ninety
nivå • *n* level

noen • *pron* anyone • *det* few
noenting • *pron* something
nok • *det* enough
nokså • *adv* rather
noledsagerinne • *n* date
nomen • *n* noun
non • *n* noon
nord • *n* north
norm • *n* norm
normal • *adj* normal
normalitet • *n* normality
noter • *n* music
notere • *v* book
novise • *n* novice
nukleær • *adj* nuclear
null • *n* love, zero
nullpunkt • *n* zero
numerus • *n* number
nummer • *n* fuck
ny • *adj* new
nybegynner • *n* novice
nyest • *adj* last
nyfødt • *adj* new
nygift • *adj* newlywed
nylig • *adj* recent
nysgjerrig • *adj* curious
nyte • *v* enjoy
nytte • *n* use
nytteløs • *adj* useless
nyttig • *adj* useful
næring • *n* food
næringsrik • *adj* nutritious
nærmest • *adj* next
nødsituasjon • *n* distress
nødvendigvis • *adv* necessarily
nøkkel • *n* key
nøle • *v* halt
nøre • *v* poke
nøyaktig • *adj* thorough
nøye • *adj* thorough
nåde • *n* mercy

når • *conj* as, if, when • *pron* when
nåværende • *adj* current, new

objekt • *n* object
objektiv • *adj* impartial
obligatorisk • *adj* mandatory
observere • *v* watch
offentlig • *adj* public
offer • *n* sacrifice, victim
offisiell • *adj* official
ofre • *v* sacrifice
ofte • *adv* often
og • *prep* plus
oi • *interj* oh
ok • *adj* cool
okkupasjon • *n* occupation
okse • *n* bull
olabukse • *n* jeans
olje • *n* oil
olm • *adj* furious, mad
om • *prep* about • *conj* if, whether
omdreining • *n* turn
omfang • *n* degree
omfatte • *v* comprise
omfattende • *adj* comprehensive
omfavne • *v* hug
omgrep • *n* concept
omhyggelig • *adj* meticulous
omkledningsrom • *n* toilet
omkring • *prep* about
område • *n* area

omsetning • *n* turnover
omsider • *adv* eventually
omstendelig • *adj* circumspect, circumstantial
omtale • *n* mention
omtrent • *adv* some
ond • *adj* bad, evil
onde • *n* evil
ondskap • *n* evil
opera • *n* opera
operasjon • *n* operation, surgery
opp • *adj* up
oppbevare • *v* store
oppblåsing • *n* inflation
oppdage • *v* spot
oppdatere • *v* update
oppdatering • *n* update
oppdatert • *adj* up
oppdra • *v* bring up
oppe • *adj* up
oppesen • *adj* up
oppfatte • *v* read
oppfinne • *v* invent
oppfinnsom • *adj* creative
oppfylle • *v* answer
oppføre • *v* behave
oppførsel • *n* behavior
oppgave • *n* problem
oppgi • *v* abandon
oppgrade • *v* upgrade
opphisse • *v* heat
opphisselse • *n* excitement
opplagt • *adj* obvious, transparent
opplyse • *v* light
opplyst • *adj* light
oppmerksom • *adj* alert, vigilant
oppmerksomhet • *n* awareness
oppmuntre • *v* encourage
oppnå • *v* attain, get

oppover • *prep* up
oppoverbakke • *n* slope
opprettholde • *v* maintain
oppriktig • *adj* candid, sincere
oppskrift • *n* receipt, recipe
oppsluke • *v* absorb
oppsummering • *n* abstract
oppsøke • *v* look
opptak • *n* take
opptatt • *adj* busy
opptelling • *n* ballot
oppå • *prep* upon
optimisme • *n* optimism
optimistisk • *adj* optimistic
oransje • *adj* orange
ord • *n* word
orden • *n* order
ordentlig • *adj* proper
ordinær • *adj* normal
ordlegge • *v* put
ordne • *v* arrange, fix, order
ordning • *n* order
ordre • *n* charge, order
original • *n* master
origo • *n* origin
orm • *n* snake, worm
Oslo • *n* Oslo
oss • *pron* us
oute • *n* outing
ovenfor • *adv* above
over • *adv* above • *prep* over
overall • *n* overall
overalt • *adv* everywhere
overdragelse • *n* purchase
overdrive • *v* exaggerate
overenskomst • *n* contract
overensstemmelse • *n* agreement
overflod • *n* abundance
overføre • *v* convey, wire
overføring • *n* grant

overgang • *n* transition
overgi • *v* grant
overgivenhet • *n* abandon
overgå • *v* exceed
overlate • *v* give
overleve • *v* survive
overlever • *n* survivor
overlykkelig • *phr* over the moon
overnatte • *v* sleep over
overnatting • *n* night
overraske • *v* surprise
overraskelse • *n* surprise
overreagere • *v* overreact
overrekke • *v* give, hand
overse • *v* ignore
oversette • *v* translate
overskride • *v* exceed
overskrift • *n* headline, title
overskye • *v* cloud
overstige • *v* exceed
oversvømme • *v* flood
overtale • *v* persuade
overveid • *adj* deliberate
overveie • *v* reason
overveielse • *n* deliberation
overvinne • *v* defeat, win
overvintre • *v* winter
overvåke • *v* monitor

pakke • *n* packet
pakt • *n* charter
Panama • *n* Panama
panda • *n* panda

O
P

pandabjørn • *n* panda
panel • *n* board
panikk • *n* panic
panne • *n* pan
pannelugg • *n* bang
panorere • *v* pan
papegøye • *n* parrot
papir • *adj* paper • *n* sheet
pappa • *n* dad, father
paradis • *n* heaven
parallell • *adj* parallel
parallelt • *adv* parallel
paraply • *n* umbrella
parat • *adj* ready
park • *n* garden
parlament • *n* parliament
parti • *n* leg
partikkel • *n* particle
partiskhet • *n* bias
partitur • *n* score
pasient • *n* patient
pass • *n* pace
passasje • *n* transit
passe • *v* go
passende • *adj* appropriate, proper, suitable
passere • *v* pass
passiv • *n* bottom • *adj* passive
passivt • *adv* passively
pasta • *n* pasta
pause • *n* half time, pause
peanøtt • *n* peanut
Pekin • *n* Beijing
Peking • *n* Beijing
pelikan • *n* pelican
pen • *adj* fine, nice, pretty
pendel • *n* pendulum
pengepung • *n* purse
penger • *n* cash
pensjon • *n* pension
pensjonat • *n* pension

pepper • *n* pepper
perfekt • *adj* perfect • *adv* perfectly
periode • *n* period
permanent • *adv* permanently
persisk • *adj* Persian
personale • *n* staff
personell • *n* personnel
Peru • *n* Peru
pese • *v* gasp
petroleum • *n* oil
piano • *n* piano
pik • *n* pike
pike • *n* domestic
pikekyss • *n* kiss
pikk • *n* prick
pil • *n* arrow
pilke • *v* pick
pine • *n* pain
pingvin • *n* penguin
pinlig • *adj* awkward
pirat • *n* pirate
piratkopiere • *v* pirate
piratkopiert • *adj* pirate
piraya • *n* piranha
pirke • *v* poke
pirkete • *adj* picky
pisk • *n* whip
plage • *v* bother
plagsom • *v* annoying
plakat • *n* bill
plan • *adj* plane
plane • *v* plane
planlegge • *v* plan
plass • *n* place, room
plassere • *v* place, position, set
plassering • *n* position
plassholder • *n* placeholder
plastikk • *adj* plastic
plate • *n* plate
plettere • *v* plate

P

plikt • *n* duty
plugg • *n* plug
plukke • *v* pick, pluck
pluss • *n* addition • *prep* plus
plyndre • *v* sack
plystre • *v* whistle
pløse • *n* tongue
poengsum • *n* score
pol • *n* pole
pomfri • *n* chip
populær • *adj* cool
port • *n* gate, port
porte • *v* port
portefølje • *n* portfolio
porting • *n* port
portvin • *n* port
pose • *n* bag
posere • *v* pose
posisjon • *n* place, position
posisjonere • *v* position
post • *n* function
pot • *n* weed
potetgull • *n* chip
prakt • *n* glory
praktisk • *adj* convenient
prat • *n* chat, talk
predikant • *n* preacher
predikere • *v* forecast
preke • *v* talk
presentasjon • *n* introduction
presidentembete • *n* presidency
presidentperiode • *n* presidency
press • *n* hurry
presse • *v* squeeze
preteritum • *n* past
prikk • *n* spot
primærfaktor • *n* prominence
prior • *n* prior

pris • *n* charge, glory, price, value
problem • *n* issue
produksjon • *n* direction
produkt • *n* product
produsere • *v* put out
proff • *n* pro
program • *n* application, broadcast, program, show
programmeringsspråk • *n* language
programpost • *n* event
programvare • *n* software
prominens • *n* prominence
promp • *n* wind
prompt • *adj* prompt • *adv* promptly
prompte • *adj* prompt • *adv* promptly
prosent • *n* rate
protest • *n* objection
protestere • *v* protest
protokoll • *n* minute
provins • *n* province
provosere • *v* provoke
prylestokk • *n* switch
prøve • *v* attempt, try • *n* sample
prøvekanin • *n* guinea pig
psykologi • *n* psychology
publikum • *n* audience
publisere • *v* publish
pudre • *v* powder
pule • *v* bone, fuck
pulverisere • *v* powder
pund • *n* pound
pung • *n* purse
punk • *n* punk
punker • *n* punk
punkt • *n* point
punktum • *n* period

punsle • *v* chase
pupill • *n* pupil
pupp • *n* tit
pur • *adj* pure
purk • *n* cop, pig
puste • *v* breathe
pute • *n* pad, pillow
putte • *v* set
pynting • *n* toilet
pysete • *adj* squeamish
pæl • *n* pale
pønk • *n* punk
pønker • *n* punk
på • *prep* on, upon
påbegynne • *v* commence
påfølgende • *adj* adjacent
påkledning • *n* dress
påle • *n* pale, stake
pålitelig • *n* trust
påskynde • *v* accelerate
påspandere • *v* treat
påspandering • *n* treat
påstand • *n* claim
påtvinge • *v* force

Qatar • *n* Qatar

rabatt • *n* discount
radmager • *adj* scrawny
rakett • *n* rocket
ramme • *n* frame • *v* hit, strike
rammeverk • *n* frame
rand • *n* border
rar • *adj* funny, strange
ras • *n* slide
rase • *v* rage
rask • *adj* fast, quick, rapid
raskt • *adv* fast
raspe • *v* grind
ravn • *n* raven
ravnsort • *adj* raven
ravnsvart • *adj* raven
redaktør • *n* editor
redd • *adj* afraid, scared
redde • *v* save
rede • *adj* ready
redegjørelse • *n* account
redigere • *n* edit
redning • *n* save
redsel • *n* horror
redskap • *n* instrument
reduksjon • *n* reduction
redusere • *v* reduce
reell • *adj* actual
referat • *n* abstract
regelmessig • *adj* regular
region • *n* belt, region
regjere • *v* reign
regn • *n* rain
regne • *v* consider, rain
regning • *n* account
regnskapskontroll • *n* audit
regnvær • *n* rain
regruppere • *v* rally
regulering • *n* regulation
reise • *v* erect, go, journey, travel, trip
reisning • *n* erection

P
Q
R

rekke • *n* chain, series • *v* reach, suffice
rekkefølge • *n* order
rekkverk • *n* rail
reklame • *n* commercial
rektor • *n* head
relevant • *adj* relevant
religiøs • *adj* religious
ren • *adj* clear, pure, sweet
rente • *n* interest
reparasjon • *n* fix, repair
reparere • *v* repair
reparering • *n* repair
reporter • *n* journalist
representere • *v* pose, represent
resept • *n* prescription
reservasjon • *n* reserve
reservat • *n* reserve
reservefond • *n* reserve
reservere • *v* book, reserve
reservering • *n* reserve
reservert • *adj* cool, reserved
reserverthet • *n* reserve
reservetropp • *n* reserve
resignere • *v* resign
resistans • *n* resistance
resonnere • *v* reason, think
respekt • *n* regard
restaurant • *n* restaurant
resultat • *n* result
resumé • *n* summary
retning • *n* direction
retningslinje • *n* guideline
rett • *n* course, plate
rev • *n* fox
revisjon • *n* audit
Reykjavik • *n* Reykjavik
Reykjavík • *n* Reykjavik
ri • *v* ride
ribbe • *v* pluck

rike • *n* realm
riktig • *adj* correct, proper
ring • *n* ring
ringe • *v* ring
ringing • *n* bell
ringmerke • *v* band
risa • *n* rise
risikere • *v* dare
risiko • *n* stake
risp • *n* scratch
riste • *v* rock, shake
rive • *v* grind
ro • *n* silence
roe • *v* silence, still
rokke • *n* ray
rolig • *adj* cool, quiet
rolle • *n* part, place, role
rom • *n* chamber, room, space
Romania • *n* Romania
romkamerat • *n* roommate
rompe • *n* behind, can
rop • *n* shout
rope • *v* shout, yell
rote • *v* root
rubin • *n* ruby
rullestol • *n* wheelchair
rumpe • *n* ass, butt
rund • *adj* round
rundt • *adv* about
Russland • *n* Russia
ruste • *v* rust
rute • *n* course, route
rutenett • *n* grid
Rwanda • *n* Rwanda
ry • *n* name
rygg • *n* back, ridge, spine
ryggrad • *n* backbone, spine
rykte • *n* rumor
rynke • *n* wrinkle
rype • *n* bird
ryste • *v* rock

R

ræv • *n* ass
rød • *adj* red
rødlig • *adj* red
rødme • *v* blush, color
røre • *n* mess • *v* move, touch
røske • *v* pluck
røyk • *n* smoke
rå • *adj* rude
råd • *n* advice
råde • *v* advise
rådgiver • *n* advisor
rådyr • *n* deer
råkjøre • *v* speed

safe • *n* safe
sage • *v* saw
sake • *n* sake
saker • *n* stuff
saksøke • *v* charge
sakte • *adv* slowly
salat • *n* salad
salt • *n* salt
salte • *v* salt
samarbeid • *n* collaboration
samarbeide • *v* collaborate, cooperate
samfunn • *n* society
samhandling • *n* interaction
samle • *v* round up
samlet • *adv* together
samling • *n* compilation
samme • *adj* very
sammendrag • *n* abstract
sammenfatning • *n* abstract

sammenlignbar • *adj* comparable
sammenligne • *v* compare
sammenligning • *n* comparison
sammenpresse • *v* crush
sammensetning • *n* composition
sammenskriving • *adj* solid
sammensmelting • *n* fusion
sammenstille • *v* join
sammenstøt • *n* crash
sammentrekke • *v* contract
sammentrekning • *n* contraction
sammentrykke • *v* crush
sample • *n* sample
samstundes • *adj* simultaneous
samtale • *n* talk
samtidig • *adj* simultaneous • *adv* simultaneously
samtykke • *n* agreement
sandfarget • *n* sand • *adj* sandy
sandstrand • *n* sand
sanksjon • *n* sanction
sanksjonere • *v* sanction
sann • *adj* proper, true
sannsynlig • *adj* likely
sannsynlighet • *n* chance
sans • *n* sense
satelitt • *n* satellite
Saturn • *n* Saturn
sau • *n* sheep
savne • *v* miss
scene • *n* scene, scenery, stage
screwdriver • *n* screwdriver
se • *v* look
sebrastripe • *n* pedestrian crossing
sedvane • *n* habit
segl • *n* seal
seier • *n* win

R
S

seiersmargin • *n* majority
seil • *n* sail
seile • *v* sail
seilende • *adj* sailing
seiltur • *n* sail
sein • *adj* late
seks • *num* six
seksten • *num* sixteen
seksti • *num* sixty
seksualslave • *n* slave
seksuell • *adj* sexy
sekund • *n* second
sekundant • *n* second
sel • *n* seal
selge • *v* sell
selskap • *n* concern
selsom • *adj* strange
selv • *n* self
selvbevissthet • *n* pride
selvmord • *n* suicide
selvmordsoffer • *n* suicide
selvsagt • *adv* obviously
senat • *n* senate
sende • *v* send
Senegal • *n* Senegal
senere • *adv* after, later
senest • *adj* last
seng • *n* bed
senke • *v* sink
sentral • *n* switch
sentrum • *n* center
serbisk • *adj* Serbian
serie • *n* series
seriøs • *adj* serious
seriøst • *adv* seriously
serr • *adv* seriously
servere • *v* serve
ses • *interj* goodbye
sesong • *n* season
sete • *n* seat
setning • *n* sentence

sette • *v* place, put, set
sexslave • *n* slave
sexy • *adj* hot, sexy
shake • *v* shake
shoppe • *v* shop
shopping • *n* shopping
show • *n* show
si • *v* go
side • *n* face, leg, side
sidekant • *n* edge, leg
siden • *adv* ago, then • *conj* as, since
sigarett • *n* cigarette
sigg • *n* cigarette
signa • *v* bless
signatur • *n* signature
sikker • *adj* certain, safe, secure
sikkert • *adv* surely
sikle • *v* drool
sikre • *v* protect
sikring • *n* safeguard
sikt • *n* view
siktemål • *n* goal
sile • *v* strain
sin • *det* her, his
Singapore • *n* Singapore
singel • *adj* sole
sinna • *adj* mad
sinne • *n* anger
sint • *adj* angry, mad
sirkel • *n* circle
siselere • *v* chase
sist • *adj* last, latter
sisten • *n* tag
sitere • *v* quote
sitte • *v* sit
sivilisasjon • *n* civilization
sjakk • *n* check
sjakkmatt • *interj* checkmate
sjallstykke • *n* bell
sjalu • *adj* jealous

S

sjanse • *n* chance
sjarmerende • *adj* charming
sjef • *n* head
sjekke • *v* check
sjel • *n* soul, spirit
sjenert • *adj* shy
sjette • *adj* sixth
sjokkere • *v* rock
sjokolade • *n* chocolate
sjokoladebrun • *adj* chocolate
sju • *num* seven
sjutall • *n* seven
sjømann • *n* sailor
sjøstjerne • *n* starfish
sjøtunge • *n* sole
skade • *v* hurt, injure, wound • *n* injury
skadelig • *adj* harmful, poisonous
skadet • *adj* hurt
skaffe • *v* afford
skal • *v* shall, will
skalk • *n* heel
skall • *n* peel
skalle • *n* skull
skam • *n* shame
skap • *n* locker
skape • *v* create
skapende • *adj* creative
skapning • *n* creation, creature
skarlagen • *n* scarlet
skarp • *adj* sharp
skarpsindig • *adj* clever
skatt • *n* tax, treasure
skatte • *v* value
skattelegge • *v* tax
skeiv • *adj* family
skift • *n* course
skikkelig • *adj* proper
skikket • *adj* skillful
skille • *v* separate

skillevegg • *n* wall
skinn • *n* skin
skinne • *n* rail
skisse • *n* draft
skissere • *v* draft
skit • *n* shit
skite • *v* shit
skitt • *n* dirt, filth, mute, shit
skittentøy • *n* laundry
skje • *v* happen, occur
skjeblad • *n* bowl
skjebne • *n* lot
skjebnebestemt • *adj* fatal
skjebnesvanger • *adj* fatal
skjelden • *adj* rare
skjell • *n* shell
skjelve • *v* shiver
skjemme • *v* deteriorate
skjemmes • *v* deteriorate
skjenke • *v* give
skjerf • *n* scarf
skjule • *v* conceal
skjult • *adj* secret
skjære • *v* mow
skjæring • *n* cutting
skjønne • *v* see, understand
skjørt • *n* skirt
skli • *v* slide, slip
skodde • *n* fog
skog • *n* forest
skole • *n* school
skolere • *v* school
skolisse • *n* shoelace
skolt • *n* skull
skorpion • *n* scorpion
skranglet • *adj* scrawny
skranke • *n* bar
skrape • *v* grind
skratte • *v* laugh
skrelle • *v* peel
skremt • *adj* scared

S

skribent • *n* writer
skrifte • *v* confess
skrike • *v* scream, yell
skrin • *n* box
skrinlegge • *v* abandon
skritt • *n* step
skrive • *v* pen, write
skrivebok • *n* notebook
skrivemaskin • *n* typewriter
skriver • *n* printer
skru • *v* hook, turn
skrue • *n* screw
skruing • *n* screw
skrujern • *n* screwdriver
skrutrekker • *n* screwdriver
skryt • *n* boast
skryte • *v* boast
skråning • *n* slope
skråstrek • *n* slash
skubbe • *v* push
skudd • *n* fix • *adj* hit
skue • *v* look
skueplass • *n* stage
skuffet • *adj* disappointed
skulle • *v* shall, should
skum • *n* head
skummel • *adj* eerie
skumring • *n* night
skunk • *n* skunk
skur • *n* shed
skvette • *v* jump
skvetting • *n* jump
sky • *n* heaven
skye • *v* cloud
skyfri • *adj* clear
skygge • *n* shadow • *v* tail
skyggelue • *n* cap
skyld • *n* fault
skylde • *v* blame, owe
skyskraper • *n* skyscraper
skyte • *v* shoot

skyteskive • *n* target
skyteskår • *n* loophole
skyts • *n* gun
skyttel • *n* shuttle
skytteltrafikk • *n* shuttle
skål • *n* bowl
sladder • *n* gossip
sladre • *v* gossip
slag • *n* fight, kind, stroke • *adj* hit
slager • *adj* hit
slaglengde • *n* travel
slagsmål • *n* combat
slakte • *v* pan
slange • *n* snake
slank • *adj* lean, thin
slarve • *v* gossip
sleide • *n* slide
slekt • *n* people
slem • *adj* evil
slette • *v* wipe
slibrig • *adj* filthy
slik • *adv* so, thus
slippe • *v* drop
slitsom • *adj* tiring
slokke • *v* put out
slott • *n* castle
Slovenia • *n* Slovenia
slukke • *v* put out
slurk • *n* draft
slutt • *n* end, finish • *adj* over
slutte • *v* end • *adj* quit
sluttstykke • *n* bolt
slynge • *v* sling
sløve • *v* dull
sløyd • *n* shop
slå • *v* beat, best, hit, knock, mow, slap, strike • *n* rail
slåss • *v* fight, struggle
slåsskamp • *n* fight
smak • *n* flavor, taste

smake • *v* taste
smakebit • *n* taste
smaksette • *v* season
smal • *adj* thin
smart • *adj* clever, sharp
smellvakker • *adj* gorgeous
smelte • *v* melt
smidig • *adj* agile
smil • *n* smile
smuss • *n* dirt
smutthull • *n* loophole
smøre • *v* oil
småkake • *n* biscuit
snakk • *n* talk
snakke • *v* speak, talk
snakkes • *interj* goodbye
snart • *adv* soon
snever • *adj* tight
snik • *n* sneak
snike • *v* jump, sneak
snill • *adj* kind, sweet
snitte • *v* carve
snu • *v* turn
snurre • *v* turn
snut • *n* pig
snyte • *v* cheat
snø • *n* snow
snøfall • *n* snow
sofa • *n* sofa
sokk • *n* sock
sokkel • *n* die
sol • *n* sun
solid • *adj* solid
soloppgang • *n* dawn
som • *conj* as • *prep* like • *pron* that, which
sommer • *n* summer
sonde • *n* probe
sone • *v* do
soningstid • *n* time
soper • *adj* gay

sordin • *n* mute
sorg • *n* grief
sort • *adj* black
sortere • *v* sort
sosial • *adj* social
sosialen • *n* social
sove • *v* sleep
Spania • *n* Spain
spann • *n* team
spare • *v* save
spark • *n* kick
sparke • *v* fire, foot, kick
sparken • *n* sack
spasere • *v* walk
spedbarn • *n* infant
spenning • *n* excitement, tension
spenst • *n* agility
spent • *adj* excited
spesialist • *n* specialist
spesialitet • *n* specialty
spesiell • *adj* special
spesielt • *adv* especially
spiker • *n* nail
spikre • *v* nail
spill • *n* game, leg
spinn • *n* spin
spinne • *v* spin, weave
spion • *n* agent
spionere • *v* spy
spirituell • *adj* spiritual
spiss • *n* attacker • *adj* sharp
splittende • *adj* disruptive
sporadisk • *adv* occasionally
sprang • *n* jump • *v* leap
spre • *v* spread
sprek • *adj* agile
spreking • *n* athlete
sprenge • *v* explode
sprenging • *n* blast
springe • *v* run

S

springer • *n* horse
sprosse • *n* rail
sprø • *adj* mad
språk • *n* language
stabel • *n* pile
stabil • *adj* stable
stake • *n* stake
stakefjær • *n* snake
stakk • *n* stack
stakkars • *adj* poor
stall • *n* stable
standpunkt • *n* stance
stangskudd • *n* poster
stappe • *v* stuff
starte • *v* start
stasjonere • *v* station
statistikk • *n* statistics
status • *n* status
stav • *n* pole, staff
stave • *v* spell
sted • *n* place, spot
steg • *n* step
steik • *n* steak
stein • *n* stone
steinaktig • *adj* stone
steine • *v* stone
stek • *n* steak
stemme • *n* speech • *v* vote
stemmeseddel • *n* ballot
stemming • *n* atmosphere
stemning • *n* mood
stempel • *n* die
stemple • *v* brand
stenge • *v* close
sterk • *adj* hot
stevnemøte • *n* date
stigmatisere • *v* brand
stigning • *n* slope
stikk • *n* bite, stab, sting, trick
stikke • *v* poke, stab, sting
stikkordregister • *n* index

stil • *n* style
stilig • *adj* cool
stilisere • *v* style
stille • *v* adjust, pose, set, still • *adv* silently • *adj* still
stilling • *n* function
stinkdyr • *n* skunk
stinke • *v* smell
stivne • *v* set
stjele • *v* steal
stoff • *n* cloth, material, stuff
stokk • *n* pole, stick
stokkand • *n* mallard
stolpe • *n* pale
stolt • *adj* proud
stolthet • *n* pride
stoppe • *v* halt
stor • *adj* large
storartet • *adj* excellent
storesøster • *n* sister
storeter • *n* pig
storsenter • *n* grocery
storslagen • *adj* brilliant
straff • *n* penalty, sentence
straffe • *v* punish, sanction
strand • *n* coast, sand, strand
strede • *n* alley
streik • *n* strike
streike • *v* strike
streng • *n* string
stress • *n* stress
streve • *v* strive
strid • *n* contention
stridslyst • *n* fight
stridslysten • *adj* belligerent
stridsvogn • *n* tank
strikke • *v* knit
stryke • *v* iron, strike
strykejern • *n* iron
strø • *v* scatter
strøk • *n* neighborhood, stroke

strøm • *n* burn, flow
strømme • *v* flow
strålende • *adj* brilliant
stråling • *n* radiation
studere • *v* read, study
stum • *adj* mute, silent
stund • *n* while
stundom • *adv* sometimes
stut • *n* cattle
stygg • *adj* ugly
stykke • *n* cake
styre • *n* board • *v* control, master
styreformann • *n* chairman
styrke • *n* force
stødig • *adj* sound, steadfast
støpsel • *n* plug
størkne • *v* set
støt • *v* thrust
støte • *v* knock
støtte • *n* second, support
støv • *n* dust
støvel • *n* boot
støvet • *adj* dusty
stå • *v* stand
ståsted • *n* place
subsidiær • *adj* subsidiary
substans • *n* substance
suffigere • *v* suffix
suge • *v* suck
sukk • *n* sigh
sukke • *v* sigh
sukker • *n* sugar
sukkertilsatt • *adj* sweet
sulky • *n* sulky
sum • *n* sum
sunn • *adj* good, sound
super • *adj* super
suppeskje • *n* tablespoon
sur • *adj* acid, sour, sulky
Surinam • *n* Suriname

suspekt • *adj* suspicious
suspendere • *v* suspend
sutre • *v* whine
svak • *adj* soft
svangerskap • *n* pregnancy
svar • *n* answer, reply
svare • *v* answer, reply
svart • *adj* black
Sveits • *n* Switzerland
svelg • *n* throat
sverte • *v* stain
svette • *v* sweat
svikte • *v* fail, yield
svimeslå • *v* stun
svin • *n* hog, pig
svindel • *n* fraud
svinekjøtt • *n* pork
sving • *n* turn
svinge • *v* turn
svitsj • *n* switch
syk • *adj* ill
syke • *n* sick
sykehus • *n* hospital
sykkel • *n* bicycle, bike
sympatisk • *adj* nice
syn • *n* view
syndig • *adj* sinful
synes • *v* look, think
synge • *v* sing
synke • *v* sink
synlig • *adj* visible
synspunkt • *n* opinion, view
syrlig • *adj* acidic
sysselsette • *v* busy
syte • *v* whine
sytten • *num* seventeen
sytti • *num* seventy
syv • *num* seven
syvtall • *n* seven
sær • *adj* strange
søke • *v* apply, hunt, look

S

søker • *n* applicant, seeker
søknad • *n* application
søksmål • *n* charge
søle • *n* mud
sølv • *n* silver
sønn • *n* son
sønnedatter • *n* granddaughter
søppel • *n* garbage, trash
søppelpost • *n* spam
sørgelig • *adj* sorry
sørnattergal • *n* nightingale
søsken • *n* sibling
søskenbarn • *n* cousin
søster • *n* sister
søt • *adj* cute, sweet
søtlig • *adj* sweet
søvn • *n* sleep
søvnig • *adj* sleepy
så • *adv* so, then • *v* sow
såle • *v* sole
sånn • *adv* thus
sår • *n* wound
såre • *v* injure, wound

ta • *v* take
tabell • *n* table
Tadsjikistan • *n* Tajikistan
tag • *n* tag
tagg • *n* tag
tak • *n* ceiling, roof, stroke
takbjelke • *n* timber
takk • *interj* thanks
takke • *v* thank
takse • *v* taxi

taksere • *v* value
tale • *n* speech
talent • *n* talent
tall • *n* rate
tankefull • *adj* pensive
tanks • *n* tank
tann • *n* tooth
tante • *n* aunt
tappe • *v* tap
tappekran • *n* tap
tapt • *adj* lost
tarm • *n* bowel
tast • *n* key
tastatur • *n* keyboard
tau • *n* cord
taushet • *n* silence
tavle • *n* board
te • *n* tea
teater • *n* theater
tegneserie • *n* comic
teknisk • *adj* technical • *adv* technically
teknologi • *n* technology
tekst • *n* lyrics, text
telefon • *n* telephone
telefonere • *v* ring
temmelig • *adv* quite, rather
tempo • *n* time
tendens • *n* tendency
tenke • *v* think
tenker • *n* mind
tenne • *v* heat, light
teologi • *n* theology
teoretisk • *adj* mathematical
teori • *n* theory
teppe • *n* blanket, throw
terminere • *v* end
terning • *n* die
terpe • *v* drill
terskel • *n* threshold
tese • *n* thesis

testament • *n* will
testamentere • *v* will
teve • *n* TV
thanksgiving • *n* Thanksgiving
ti • *num* ten
tid • *n* time
tidsskrift • *n* journal, magazine
tidvis • *adv* sometimes
til • *prep* for, till, to
tilbake • *adv* back
tilbakeholdenhet • *n* reserve
tilby • *v* offer
tilbøyelig • *adj* poised
tilbøyelighet • *n* inclination
tildele • *v* grant
tildeling • *n* grant
tilfeldig • *adj* accidental,
    arbitrary, casual, random
tilfeldigheter • *n* chance
tilfelle • *n* occurrence
tilfelleleg • *adj* random
tilfellelig • *adj* random
tilfreds • *adj* content, satisfied
tilfredsstille • *v* answer, satisfy
tilføye • *v* enclose
tilgang • *n* access
tilgi • *v* excuse, forgive
tilkalle • *v* summon
tillate • *v* allow, sanction
tillatelse • *n* permission,
    sanction
tillegg • *n* addition
tillit • *n* trust
tilltale • *n* indictment
tilnærmelsesmåte • *n*
    approach
tilpasse • *v* appropriate
tilstand • *n* condition, state
tilstrekkelig • *adj* adequate •
    det enough
tilstundelse • *n* approach

tilstå • *v* confess
tilsynelatende • *adv* apparently
tiltale • *v* please, style
tiltaleform • *n* style
tiltalende • *adj* attractive
tiltrekkende • *adj* attractive,
    magnetic
tilvenne • *v* condition
tilværelse • *n* being, existence
time • *n* hour
timeplan • *n* schedule
ting • *n* object, parliament,
    stuff, thing
tinn • *n* tin
tirsdag • *n* Tuesday
tiss • *n* water
tisse • *v* water
tiår • *n* decade
tjene • *v* make, serve
tjenestejente • *n* domestic
tjue • *num* twenty
tjuende • *adj* twentieth
to • *num* two
toalett • *n* toilet
tobakk • *n* tobacco
tog • *n* train
togn • *n* silence
Tokyo • *n* Tokyo
tolerere • *v* tolerate
tolk • *n* interpreter
tolv • *num* twelve
tom • *adj* empty
tomhet • *n* emptiness
tomme • *n* inch
tommeskrue • *n* thumb
tomt • *n* garden, property
tone • *n* tone
tonefall • *n* accent
topp • *n* head
toppstrøk • *n* finish
tordne • *v* thunder

torp • *n* village
torsdag • *n* Thursday
torsk • *n* cod
tortur • *n* torture
torturere • *v* torture
tosk • *n* ass, fool
totalt • *adv* entirely
trafikk • *n* traffic
traktat • *n* contract, treaty
trang • *n* urge
trangsynt • *adj* narrow-minded
transparent • *adj* transparent
trapp • *n* stair
traust • *adj* steadfast
travel • *adj* busy
travelhet • *n* hurry
traversere • *v* weave
tre • *num* three • *n* tree, wood
tredoble • *v* triple
treffe • *v* hit, nail, place
treffvirkning • *n* impact
trekk • *n* draft, move, trait
trekke • *v* pull
trene • *v* exercise, train
trenge • *v* need
trengsel • *n* jam
treningsøkt • *n* workout
treslag • *n* wood
tresort • *n* wood
tretten • *num* thirteen
treverk • *n* wood
trevirke • *n* timber
tri • *num* three
trick • *n* trick
trikk • *n* trick
triks • *n* trick
trin • *n* step
trinn • *n* grade, stair
trist • *adj* sad, sullen
tro • *v* believe, think • *n* faith • *adj* faithful, true

troende • *adj* faithful
trofast • *adj* true
trommeslager • *n* drummer
trommis • *n* drummer
tropp • *n* troop
trygg • *adj* safe
trygt • *adv* safely, surely
trykk • *n* accent
trykke • *v* print, squeeze
trykknapp • *n* button
trykkplate • *n* plate
trylleformel • *n* spell
trøe • *n* pole
trøtt • *adj* sleepy
tråd • *n* thread
Tsjad • *n* Chad
tulle • *v* joke, kid
tullete • *adj* silly
tulling • *n* ass, fool
tunge • *n* tongue
tur • *n* turn
turisme • *n* tourism
turist • *n* tourist
tusen • *num* thousand
Tuvalu • *n* Tuvalu
TV • *n* TV
tvang • *n* force
tvangsinnlegge • *v* section
tvette • *v* wash
tvil • *n* doubt
tvinge • *v* compel, force
tyding • *n* meaning
tyende • *n* domestic
tygge • *n* bite • *v* chew
tykktarm • *n* bowel
tynn • *adj* scrawny, thin
Tyrkia • *n* Turkey
tyve • *num* twenty
tømme • *v* empty
tømmer • *n* timber
tørke • *v* dry

tørne • *v* turn
tørr • *adj* dry
tørst • *adj* thirsty
tørste • *n* thirst
tøy • *n* material
tøyse • *v* kid
tå • *n* digit, toe
tåke • *n* fog
tåkelegge • *v* fog
tåle • *v* afford, bear, stand, take, tolerate
tårer • *n* tear
tårnfalk • *n* kestrel

uansett • *adv* anyway
uavgjort • *n* draw
ubarmhjertig • *adj* ruthless
ubehag • *n* distress
ubehagelig • *adj* bad • *adv* terrible
uenig • *v* disagree
uenighet • *n* dispute
uforskamma • *adj* naughty
uforskammet • *adj* rude
ufyselig • *adj* obnoxious
ugress • *n* weed
ugunstig • *adj* adverse
uheldig • *adj* inappropriate, unfortunate
uhensiktsmessig • *adj* adverse
uhørt • *adj* outrageous
ukjent • *adj* strange
uklarhet • *n* fog
Ukraina • *n* Ukraine

ulik • *adj* different, unlike
ulike • *adj* odd, various
ultimat • *adj* ultimate
umoderne • *adj* dated
under • *prep* beneath, under
underfull • *adj* wonderful
underhold • *n* keep
underjordisk • *adj* underground
underkue • *v* cow
underskrift • *n* signature
underskudd • *n* deficit
understreke • *v* emphasize
undersøke • *v* examine, probe
undervise • *v* teach
undres • *v* wonder
ung • *adj* small, young
Ungarn • *n* Hungary
ungdom • *n* kid, youth
unge • *n* kid
unik • *adj* unique
union • *n* union
univers • *n* universe
unnateke • *conj* except
unnateki • *conj* except
unngå • *v* avoid, cheat, escape, except

unnkomme • *v* escape
unnskyld • *interj* sorry
unnskylde • *v* excuse
unnskyldning • *n* excuse
unnslippe • *v* escape
unnta • *v* except
unntatt • *conj* but, except • *prep* save
unnvikende • *adj* evasive
unormal • *adj* abnormal
unyttig • *adj* useless
unødvendig • *adj* unnecessary
upartisk • *adj* candid, impartial
upassende • *adj* inappropriate
ur • *n* watch

uriktig • *adj* wrong
uro • *n* concern, mobile
uroe • *v* worry
usaltet • *adj* sweet
Usbekistan • *n* Uzbekistan
uskarphet • *n* fog
uskikkelig • *adj* naughty
uskikket • *adj* inappropriate
usynlig • *adj* invisible
ut • *adv* out
utbrudd • *n* access
utdanne • *v* school
utdatert • *adj* dated
utdrag • *n* abstract
utdype • *v* expand
ute • *adv* out • *adj* up
utelukke • *v* ban, exclude
uten • *adj* free
utenomjordisk • *adj* alien
utestående • *adj* outstanding
utfall • *n* result
utfordre • *v* dare
utfordring • *n* challenge, dare, problem
utforske • *v* explore, probe
utgående • *adj* up
utgått • *adj* dated
utheve • *v* highlight
utholde • *v* absorb
utilfreds • *adj* sullen
utkast • *n* draft
utlade • *v* discharge
utlegg • *n* attachment
utmerket • *adj* excellent
utnevne • *v* name
utnytte • *v* exploit
utover • *prep* above
utpresning • *n* blackmail
utpressing • *n* blackmail
utprøve • *v* try out

utropstegn • *n* exclamation mark
utrøttelig • *adj* indefatigable
utseende • *n* look
utsending • *n* broadcast
utside • *prep* outside
utsikt • *n* view
utskeielse • *n* excess
utskjelling • *n* abuse
utskrive • *v* discharge, draft
utskrivning • *n* discharge
utstråling • *n* radiation
utstå • *v* bear
utstående • *adj* outstanding
utsyn • *n* view
uttale • *n* accent, pronunciation • *v* pronounce
uttrykk • *n* expression, look
uttrykke • *v* express
utvide • *v* expand
utvilsomt • *adv* definitely
utvisning • *n* ban, discharge
utålelig • *adj* obnoxious
uvenn • *n* enemy

vakker • *adj* pretty, sweet
vaksinering • *n* vaccination
vakt • *n* watch
valg • *n* choice, election, pick
valgbar • *adj* eligible
valgliste • *n* ballot
valgmulighet • *n* option
valgt • *adj* elect
vandre • *v* walk

vandring • *n* hike
vane • *n* habit
vanlig • *adj* common, general, normal
vanligvis • *adv* usually
vann • *n* water
vannføring • *n* discharge
vannklosett • *n* toilet
vanskelig • *adj* difficult
vant • *n* board
vante • *n* glove
Vanuatu • *n* Vanuatu
varemerke • *n* brand, trademark
varer • *n* shopping
variabel • *adj* variable
varierende • *adj* variable
varm • *adj* hot, warm
varme • *n* heat
varmt • *adj* hot
varsel • *n* alert
varsle • *v* alert
vaske • *v* wash
vaskerom • *n* laundry
vater • *n* level
vatret • *adj* level
ved • *prep* by, upon • *n* wood
vedde • *v* bet
veddemål • *n* bet
vedlegge • *v* enclose
vedlikeholde • *v* maintain
vedtak • *n* resolution
veg • *n* road
vei • *n* road
veileder • *n* advisor
veiledning • *n* instruction
vekk • *adv* out
vekke • *v* wake
vekst • *n* growth
vekt • *n* balance
veldig • *adv* most, really, very
velegnet • *adj* appropriate

velge • *v* name, pick
velkomst • *n* welcome
vellyst • *n* pleasure
veloppdragent • *adj* proper
veloverveid • *adj* deliberate
velsigne • *v* bless
vemmelig • *adj* ugly
vende • *v* turn
vending • *n* turn
venn • *n* friend
venninne • *n* friend
vennlig • *adj* kind, sweet
venstre • *adj* left
venstresiden • *n* left
vente • *n* waiting
ventende • *n* waiter
verb • *n* verb
verd • *n* value
verden • *n* world
verdi • *n* value
verdsette • *v* appreciate, value
verk • *n* work
verksted • *n* workshop
verktøy • *n* tool
verne • *v* defend, protect
verneplikt • *n* draft
vers • *n* verse
versjon • *n* version
versus • *prep* versus
vesen • *n* being
vesentligen • *adv* substantially
vestlig • *adj* western
vett • *n* wit
vev • *n* weave
veve • *v* weave
vid • *adj* full • *adv* wide
vidd • *n* wit
vidgjeten • *adj* renowned
vidt • *adv* wide
vie • *v* wed
vifte • *n* fan

V

viktig ● *adj* important
vil ● *v* will
vilje ● *n* will
vilkår ● *n* condition, term
vilkårlig ● *adj* arbitrary
vill ● *adj* wild
ville ● *v* want, will
vin ● *n* wine
vind ● *n* wind
vindrue ● *n* grape
vinke ● *v* wave
vinne ● *v* win
virke ● *v* go, work
virkelig ● *adj* actual, real
virkning ● *n* impact
virkningsfull ● *adj* effective
virksom ● *adj* effective
vis ● *adj* wise
visdom ● *n* wisdom
vise ● *v* show
viser ● *n* indicator
viske ● *v* wipe
visning ● *n* view
viss ● *adj* certain
visse ● *det* certain ● *pron* some
visst ● *det* certain
visstnok ● *adv* allegedly
visum ● *n* visa
vital ● *adj* vital
vite ● *v* know
vitne ● *v* evidence ● *n* witness
vitneforklaring ● *n* evidence
vitneutsagn ● *n* evidence
vits ● *n* joke, laugh
vittig ● *adj* witty
vogn ● *n* car, carriage, wagon
vokal ● *adj* vocal
vokale ● *adj* vocal
vokse ● *v* expand, grow
voksen ● *n* adult ● *adj* mature
voldsom ● *adj* fierce, vast

voldta ● *v* abuse, take ● *n* assault
voldtekt ● *n* abuse
voll ● *n* wall
vond ● *adj* ugly
vrak ● *n* wreck
vrang ● *adj* wrong
vri ● *v* twist
vridning ● *n* turn
vulkan ● *n* volcano
vurdere ● *v* consider, contemplate, value
værelse ● *n* room
våge ● *v* dare
våghals ● *n* daredevil
våken ● *adj* alert
våkne ● *v* wake up
vår ● *det* our ● *n* spring
våt ● *adj* wet
vått ● *adj* wet

western ● *n* western
whisky ● *n* whiskey

yard ● *n* yard
ydmyk ● *adj* humble
yeah ● *part* yeah

yes • *interj* yes
ymse • *adj* various
yndlings • *adj* favourite
yngling • *n* youth
ynkelig • *adj* puny
yrke • *n* occupation
yte • *v* yield
ytterkant • *n* border
ytterside • *n* outside

æra • *n* period
ære • *n* glory
ærede • *adj* dear

ødelegge • *v* deteriorate
ødelegges • *v* go
øh • *interj* uh
øke • *v* increase, up
økonomi • *n* economics
økonomisering • *n* saving
øl • *n* beer
ønske • *n* desire, will • *v* want
ørefik • *n* slap
ørken • *n* desert
ørn • *n* eagle
øskje • *n* box

øve • *v* train
øvelse • *n* rehearsal
øving • *n* rehearsal
øvre • *adj* upper
øyeblikk • *n* minute, second

å • *interj* oh • *n* river
åker • *n* field
ål • *n* eel
åle • *v* worm
ålreit • *adj* all right
ånd • *n* mind, spirit
ånde • *v* breathe
åndelig • *adj* spiritual
åndrik • *adj* witty
åpen • *adj* free
åpenbar • *adj* manifest, transparent
åpenbaring • *n* revelation, vision
åpenbart • *adv* obviously
åpne • *v* open
åpnes • *v* open
årsak • *n* cause, factor
årsdag • *n* anniversary
årskull • *n* class
årstid • *n* season
årti • *n* decade
ås • *n* hill
åsrygg • *n* ridge
åtte • *num* eight
åtti • *num* eighty

Pronunciation

Consonants

IPA	Example	Equivalent
b	bil	bee
ç	kjip	huge
d	dag	day
ɖ	sardin	*retroflex* d
ʁd	sardin	*French* corde
f	fot	foot
g	god	good
h	hatt	hat
j	jojo	yoyo
k	kafé	coffee
l	lake	lack
ḷ	Abel	little*
ɭ	Karl	*retroflex* l
ʁl	Karl	*French* Arles
m	man	man
n	natt	night
ṇ	natten	chosen
ɳ	barn	*retroflex* n
ʁn	barn	*French* Marne
ɳ̩	baren	-
ŋ	ting	thing
p	pappa	papa

r	år	*American* latter
ʁ	år	*Scottish* loch
ʈ	Vålerenga	*retroflex American* latter
s	sabel	sabre
ʂ	sjø, torsdag	*retroflex* shoe
ʁs	torsdag	*French* Corse
t	tirsdag	time
ʈ	parti	*retroflex* t
ʁt	parti	*French* carte
v	vaktel	vat

Vowels

IPA	Example	Equivalent
ɑ	fast	art
ɑː	mat	bra, car
æ	fersk	trap
æː	ære	*Australian* mad
ɛ	helle	set
eː	hel	*Scottish* save
ɪ	sill	hill
iː	i	need
ɔ	åtte	off
oː	mål	goal
œ	nøtt	*like* bet
øː	dø	*Scottish* save
ʁ	ond	put
uː	bot	fool
ʉ	full	*Australian* goose
ʉː	ful	*Australian* choose
ʏ	nytt	*like* hit
yː	syl	*like* leave
ɑɪ	kai	*Australian* price
æɪ	bein	*Australian* day
æʉ	hauk	*Australian* now
ɛɪ	tape	day
ɔʏ	boikott	boy
œʏ	røyk	*Scottish* house
ʉɪ	hui	to eternity

ə | pâle   about

Irregular English Verbs

inf.	sp.	pp.	inf.	sp.	pp.
arise	arose	arisen	buy	bought	bought
awake	awoke	awoken	can	could	-
be	was	been	cast	cast	cast
bear	bore	borne	catch	caught	caught
beat	beat	beaten	choose	chose	chosen
become	became	become	cleave	cleft	cleft
beget	begot	begotten	come	came	come
begin	began	begun	cost	cost	cost
bend	bent	bent	creep	crept	crept
bet	bet	bet	crow	crowed	crew
bid	bade	bidden	cut	cut	cut
bide	bade	bided	deal	dealt	dealt
bind	bound	bound	dig	dug	dug
bite	bit	bitten	do	did	done
bleed	bled	bled	draw	drew	drawn
blow	blew	blown	dream	dreamt	dreamt
break	broke	broken	drink	drank	drunk
breed	bred	bred	drive	drove	driven
bring	brought	brought	dwell	dwelt	dwelt
build	built	built	eat	ate	eaten
burn	burnt	burnt	fall	fell	fallen
burst	burst	burst	feed	fed	fed
bust	bust	bust	feel	felt	felt

inf.	sp.	pp.	inf.	sp.	pp.
fight	fought	fought	mow	mowed	mown
find	found	found	pay	paid	paid
flee	fled	fled	pen	pent	pent
fling	flung	flung	plead	pled	pled
fly	flew	flown	prove	proved	proven
forbid	forbad	forbid	quit	quit	quit
forget	forgot	forgotten	read	read	read
forsake	forsook	forsaken	rid	rid	rid
freeze	froze	frozen	ride	rode	ridden
get	got	got	ring	rang	rung
give	gave	given	rise	rose	risen
go	went	gone	run	ran	run
grind	ground	ground	saw	sawed	sawn
grow	grew	grown	say	said	said
hang	hung	hung	see	saw	seen
have	had	had	seek	sought	sought
hear	heard	heard	sell	sold	sold
hide	hid	hidden	send	sent	sent
hit	hit	hit	set	set	set
hold	held	held	sew	sewed	sewn
hurt	hurt	hurt	shake	shook	shaken
keep	kept	kept	shall	should	-
kneel	knelt	knelt	shear	sheared	shorn
know	knew	known	shed	shed	shed
lay	laid	laid	shine	shone	shone
lead	led	led	shit	shit	shit
lean	leant	leant	shoe	shod	shod
leap	leapt	leapt	shoot	shot	shot
learn	learnt	learnt	show	showed	shown
leave	left	left	shred	shred	shred
lend	lent	lent	shrink	shrank	shrunk
let	let	let	shut	shut	shut
lie	lay	lain	sing	sang	sung
light	lit	lit	sink	sank	sunk
lose	lost	lost	sit	sat	sat
make	made	made	slay	slew	slain
may	might	-	sleep	slept	slept
mean	meant	meant	slide	slid	slid
meet	met	met	sling	slung	slung
melt	melted	molten	slink	slunk	slunk

inf.	sp.	pp.	inf.	sp.	pp.
slit	slit	slit	wed	wed	wed
smell	smelt	smelt	weep	wept	wept
smite	smote	smitten	wet	wet	wet
sow	sowed	sown	win	won	won
speak	spoke	spoken	wind	wound	wound
speed	sped	sped	wring	wrung	wrung
spell	spelt	spelt	write	wrote	written
spend	spent	spent			
spill	spilt	spilt			
spin	spun	spun			
spit	spat	spat			
split	split	split			
spoil	spoilt	spoilt			
spread	spread	spread			
spring	sprang	sprung			
stand	stood	stood			
steal	stole	stolen			
stick	stuck	stuck			
sting	stung	stung			
stink	stank	stunk			
stride	strode	stridden			
strike	struck	struck			
string	strung	strung			
strive	strove	striven			
swear	swore	sworn			
sweat	sweat	sweat			
sweep	swept	swept			
swell	swelled	swollen			
swim	swam	swum			
swing	swung	swung			
take	took	taken			
teach	taught	taught			
tear	tore	torn			
tell	told	told			
throw	threw	thrown			
thrust	thrust	thrust			
tread	trod	trodden			
wake	woke	woken			
wear	wore	worn			
weave	wove	woven			

Printed in Great Britain
by Amazon